FOREVER FAITH

FOREVER FAITH

The Abe Cruz Story

Mindset of Champions

By Abe Cruz

and

Jeanette Windle

FOREVER FAITH

Copyright © 2020 by Abe Cruz and Jeanette Windle

All rights reserved. No part of this book shall be reproduced or transmitted in any form or by any means, electronic, mechanical, magnetic, photographic including photocopying, recording or by any information storage and retrieval system, without prior written permission of the publisher. No patent liability is assumed with respect to the use of the information contained herein. Although every precaution has been taken in the preparation of this book, the publisher and author assume no responsibility for errors or omissions. Neither is any liability assumed for damages resulting from the use of the information contained herein.

ISBN: 978-1-7358889-0-3 English print
ISBN: 978-1-7358889-1-0 English ebook
ISBN: 978-1-7358889-2-7 Spanish print
ISBN: 978-1-7358889-3-4 Spanish ebook

Forever Faith
Broken Arrow, OK
www.foreverfaith.com

Translation (English to Spanish) by Keila Ochoa Harris
Cover designed by Jesty Leparto (jhezz31), **www.99designs.com**
Cover photos of Abe by Kike San Martin Photography
Book and EBook designed and formatted by EBook Listing Services,
www.ebooklistingservices.com

Publisher's Cataloging-in-Publication Data
Names: Cruz, Abe, author. | Windle, Jeanette, author.
Title: Forever faith : the Abe Cruz story , mindset of champions / by Abe Cruz and Jeanette Windle.
Description: Broken Arrow, OK: Forever Faith, 2020.
Identifiers: LCCN 2020919221 | ISBN 9781735888903
Subjects: LCSH Cruz, Abe. | Christian biography. | Businessmen--Biography. | Trust in God--Christianity. | BISAC BIOGRAPHY & AUTOBIOGRAPHY / Personal Memoirs | BIOGRAPHY & AUTOBIOGRAPHY / Religious | RELIGIOUS / Christian Living / Inspirational
Classification: LCC BR1700.2 .C78 2020 | DDC 248.84--dc23

FOREVER FAITH

1 3 5 7 9 10 8 6 4 2
Printed in the United States of America

DEDICATION

First of all, I dedicate this book to God, my true heavenly Father, who gave me a second chance to proclaim his message of faith to the whole world.

I also dedicate it to **my loving mother**, who has been my strength. She educated and molded me to be the man I am today. I love you mama!

I also dedicate this book to Pops, **Fred Bassett**. I could write a whole thank you book. You have been an angel sent by GOD and you have always been a blessing in my life and that of my family. The only explanation is that GOD brought us together for this mission to inspire and motivate the world. Also to Pops's wife, **Janet**, thank you for being by our side through thick and thin to this day. I love you both!

Finally, I dedicate this book to my amazing, supportive and beautiful wife **Ha**, who has sacrificed so much for us to get to this moment, and to our two children, **Justin** and **Joshua**. They have witnessed this journey from the beginning, and it has been a blessing to have them by my side. I love them very much!

ACKNOWLEDGEMENTS

A special thanks for being part of my life and my journey:

To my brother **David**. Thank you for being such an amazing and supportive brother. You have always been there for me through thick and thin, and I will never forget your hard work and sacrifice.

To my sister **Marta**. Thank you for always being there for me.

To **Ken Mendoza**, a volunteer for Hermano Mayor's organization, and his wife **Rose**, for introducing us to sports and giving us so much love.

To **Oscar Cepeida**, who taught me at eleven what it means to have the mentality of a champion, and to his wife **Ofelia** and their children **Olivia**, **Orlando**, **Omar** and **Oliver** who opened the doors of their home to me.

To **Hugo Cepeida**, his wife **Amelia**, and their children **André** and **Abel**, who treated me like part of their family and were another blessing in my youth.

To **Phil** and **Dolores Corona**, my head coach in the East Los Angeles Bobcats football program, to his daughters **Erin** and **Cindy**, and his sons **Phil Jr** and **Jeff**, who were like my siblings in high school.

To **Coach Pitts** and **Coach Robbleto** of the *Pasadena Panthers*, the first organized sports team I ever played for.

To **Eli Garcia**, my seventh grade coach at *Todos los Santos Elementary*, and his son **Jessie**, who were a great influence in my life.

To **Coach Duarte** and **Coach Rafino** from *San Pablo High School*, my first year coaches who guided us to an undefeated season. Thank you for teaching me discipline, sacrifice, and work ethic.

To **Coach Visko** and **Coach Jiménez**, my junior soccer coaches, and for the many hours of training, hard work, and sacrifice that helped me to be a better player, and ultimately a better person.

Coach Marijon Ancich, who set the record for the most high school wins in California over three seasons. I was lucky to play under his tutelage.

To my basketball coach, **Randy Castillo**, who led São Paulo to its first CIF championship, and assistant coaches **Fox** and **Ertle**.

To **Coach Strop** and **Coach Miercort** of the *University of Wisconsin Stout* for believing that I could bring something valuable to their football program.

To **Jessi** and **Valerie Muñoz** for being great role models and giving me a support system.

To **Art Cacciatori**, who was there for me through a difficult time before going to prison.

To **Lonnie Tepper**, who believed I had a future in the fitness world, before I did.

To bodybuilding legend **Jay Cutler**, whose autograph gave me great encouragement while in prison.

To **Aura Duran**, for her friendship and the letters that in prison kept me optimistic and thinking about my future.

To **Joan Black**, who supported my dreams and gave me great encouragement when I was working out at the *All American Fitness* gym in Tulsa after I got out of prison.

To **Dr. Luis Arriaza**, from whom I learned a lot about how to be a successful business entrepreneur and whom I am honored to call a friend.

To **Scott Matlock**, Vice President of *10 GYM*, for his willingness to take a chance and hire me after prison to give me a fresh start in life.

To **John** and **Kathryn Helstrom**, pastor in the prison ministry of Creek County Prison in Sapulpa, Oklahoma, whose deep love for me and other prisoners greatly impacted my life.

To **José Miranda**, pastor at John Helstrom's church, who has been my friend and mentor since we met.

To **Corey Taylor**, television host and bestselling author whose faith in me and good advice led me to write this book.

To **Luz Ramírez**, for her hard work and sacrifice and for believing in the mission of *Forever Faith*. Never forget you.

To **TJ Walker**, founding member of the *Cross Colors* clothing line, who generously invested his time teaching me the clothing business and fashion design. I not only learned about clothes but how kind, considerate, generous and professional TJ is. Thank you very much, TJ.

To celebrity fitness photographer, **Noel Daganta**, who helped launch my fitness career and blessed me with my first magazine covers.

To coach **Michael Lopez** for his love and mentoring and for always being there for me through thick and thin. That is true friendship.

To **Guy Kochlani**, who encouraged me to write this book.

To **Ron Brown** for helping me see the big picture.

To **Christopher Pope** for helping me bring my visions to life through his incredible art.

To **George Steele** for his commitment and help during difficult times.

To **Marc Harper** and his wife **Ceitci** for believing in the mission of *Forever Faith* and wanting to make an impact on the world.

To **Jim Spargur** and his wife **Lalie** for seeing the vision and understanding that it is God's mission.

To many others. Your kindness and generosity has impacted and changed my life. I can't name them all, but I want to thank **Father Gallagher** of San Pablo, **Reverend B.J. Johnson**, **Dusto** the architect, **Antione Fletcher**, **Joe Shen**, **Raul Ibarra**, **Javier** and **Ron** from the *Del Mar Boys and Girls Club*, Pasadena, and everyone in the *Pasadena Panthers* organization.

Table of Contents

Introduction..1
    It Just Takes Faith

Chapter One...5
    Time to Run!

Chapter Two..11
    Not Good Enough to Stay

Chapter Three..17
    Big Brother

Chapter Four..23
    Birthing a Mindset

Chapter Five...27
    New Blessings

Chapter Six..33
    A Way Out

Chapter Seven..39
    Nothing Could Stop Me But Me!

Chapter Eight...45
    Up and Down

Chapter Nine..51
    Sidelined

Chapter Ten...57
    Hooked

Chapter Eleven...65
    Fast Cash, Fast Crash

Chapter Twelve..73
    The Good Life

Chapter Thirteen..81
    Ghosted

Chapter Fourteen..87
    Desperation and Decisions

Chapter Fifteen..93
    Soaring High

Chapter Sixteen...97
    Really Hooked!

Chapter Seventeen..103
    Out of Control

Chapter Eighteen..109
    Busted

Chapter Nineteen..115
    Guilty as Charged

Chapter Twenty...121
    Let's Make a Deal

Chapter Twenty-One..127
    Rock Bottom

Chapter Twenty-Two..135
    Prayer and Fasting

Chapter Twenty-Three...141
    New Beginning

Chapter Twenty-Four...147
    Keeping the Faith

Chapter Twenty-Five..153
    Abe 2.0

Chapter Twenty-Six..159
    New Blessings, New Challenges

Chapter Twenty-Seven...167
    Birth of a Movement

Chapter Twenty-Eight...175
    Love of My Life

Chapter Twenty-Nine...181
    Mindset of Champions

Epilogue..187
    Just Believe!

About the Authors...191

Forever Faith!..192

INTRODUCTION
IT JUST TAKES FAITH!

FAITH SAVED MY LIFE. AND BELIEVE ME, if faith can do that for me, it can save you too! Though it wasn't until I hit rock-bottom and found myself in prison at the age of twenty-five that I learned what real faith is all about.

Mindset-of-Champions faith.

Forever faith.

So let me tell you how I got there—and why I'm writing this book. My full name is Abraham Joshua Cruz, though everyone ends up calling me Abe. All three names come from the Bible. I know that was no coincidence since my mom comes from a devoutly Christian family heritage. But growing up in a gang-and-drug-infested neighborhood of Los Angeles, I knew nothing of their significance. I did know that *cruz* is Spanish for the cross on which our Lord and Savior Jesus Christ sacrificed himself for our salvation. Joshua was a great warrior who helped Moses deliver the Jewish people from slavery in Egypt and lead them into the Promised Land.

Then there's my first name. In the Bible, Abraham is called the father of faith. That was definitely not me! Sure, I believed in GOD and prayer because my mom raised me that way. But my primary focus was winning. First as an All-Star athlete from elementary school all the way into college. Then as a business entrepreneur making $5000 a week by the time I was twenty.

I wanted to be a champion. To be the best I could be. Not to help others or make a difference in this world. For myself. To get rich. To have the pretty girls. The playboy lifestyle. The bling. The fancy car, house, clothes, shoes. All the things I saw the rich and famous enjoying everywhere I looked, so why not me!

Okay, maybe to help Mom and family too. At least that's what I told myself. I was still telling myself that when a series of really bad choices put an end to my get-rich-quick lifestyle and left me serving a three-year prison sentence.

A lot of leadership development programs talk about the mindset of a champion. Self-confidence. Determination. Focus. Hard work. Pushing through the pain. Being resilient. Picking yourself up when you fall. Not letting failure define you. Staying strong. Those are all characteristics of a champion I try to live by.

> **"The mindset of champions is about becoming the very best version of yourself."** —Abe Cruz

But I've come to recognize that the real mindset of a champion is faith. Not just faith in your own strength, smarts, and talents. Faith in GOD first and believing in your own capabilities second. Not a faith either that's all about achieving your own wealth, fame, and success, but a faith that puts others first. That lives out the saying you so often hear but rarely see practiced: "What would Jesus do?"

I learned all this the hard way on my face before GOD spilling tears onto the cold concrete floor of a prison cell. Prison is an experience I wouldn't wish on my worst enemy. Prison will break you down physiologically and psychologically. I saw and experienced some terrible things there. I witnessed a lot of other prisoners completely losing their faith and hope.

But for me, prison turned out to be the biggest blessing of my life. Nothing I have today physically, spiritually, mentally, or financially would have come about without going to prison and hitting rock-bottom. Prison was my wake-up call. It scared me straight and kicked me off the wrong path I was on before it was too late.

More than that, hitting rock-bottom forced me flat on my back where all I could see was up. And when I looked up, I saw GOD. I found faith. I was also given a vision of what GOD wanted me to achieve with the rest of my life.

Literally a vision. It came during a forty-day time of fasting and prayer Mom had challenged me to do. In the vision, I was standing on a hill, just like I'd stood when I was arrested, except instead of looking down at counter-narcotics agents and drug dogs and police cruisers, I was looking out over a crowd of people as far as I could see. And I was speaking to them about faith and how much GOD loved them. Then I was in the middle of the crowd, picking up a fallen child here, helping an old man in trouble there, speaking hope to groups of young boys in juvenile detention, one scene after another of assisting others.

I also saw myself creating an inspirational movement and a faith-based clothing line, speaking on TV, being on the cover of magazines, and traveling all over the world. It was as though I was audibly hearing GOD say to me, "Just like your namesake Abraham, *m'ijo*, I am calling you to be a man of faith. If you answer my call, I am going to bless you for your faith and you are going to bless others by your faith."

What is mind-blowing is that everything I saw in my vision has come true. Starting with developing a faith-based fitness and self-development program right there in prison with fellow inmates. That was the beginning of Forever Faith, which today is not just a multi-lingual fashion and fitness brand but a mission of inspiration and motivation that is reaching people all over the world. More about that later.

The old Abe would have been all excited about climbing a new ladder of success. Now I just see opportunities to share GOD's message of faith, hope, and love. I am also so thankful to have been blessed with an incredible gorgeous wife and two wonderful sons.

So just what is Forever Faith? It's about having the mindset of a champion. It means becoming the very best person you can be in every area of life. And the root of that is putting GOD first because GOD *is* the ultimate champion. If you are following GOD and putting GOD first, you will automatically become the best version of yourself that you can be, whether physically, mentally, spiritually, etc.

I have chosen to be that person, and I hope you have too. One thing I know for sure is that I'm not the only one who has made bad choices, been in tough places, and hit rock-bottom. There are a lot of people stuck in their own tough places who are looking for guidance and advice from someone who has hit bottom and made it back out.

That's why I'm writing this book. To let people know God gives second chances. That tough times, obstacles, even our worst mistakes and failures can lead to a bright, hopeful, purpose-filled, dream-fulfilled, God -blessed future.

It just takes faith.

Forever Faith!

CHAPTER ONE
TIME TO RUN!

I WAS HALFWAY HOME AND FEELING great as the Tulsa skyline disappeared from my rearview mirror. I'd been driving more than twelve hours since leaving Columbus, Ohio, and it was now well past midnight. But with several energy drinks pumping me up, I felt energized enough to push on to my final destination—Los Angeles. Even if it meant driving thirty-plus hours straight, I could never relax until my cargo was safely handed off.

In this case, half a million in cash stowed in various hidden compartments all over the 350Z silver Nissan sports car I was driving. Payment in kind for an equivalent value of tightly-wrapped one-kilo white bricks of cocaine I'd delivered to Columbus two days back. Not that I had any worries. Maybe because at twenty-five, I didn't have the survival smarts to be appropriately nervous. Or because after eighteen months of successful round trips, including several near-encounters with law enforcement, I was feeling pretty invincible.

Big, green signs announcing exits for Oklahoma City began flashing by. I'd done this drive so many times by now I didn't even need to think about the next lane change or exit. I was thinking instead about how I'd been promised my biggest payday yet once I delivered my cargo—$35,000 return on less than a week of work. How would I spend it? Another Rolex? A weekend clubbing? A trip to Las Vegas?

Of course I'd give Mom a few hundred, maybe even thousand, towards her rent and my own room and board. Not enough to raise unwelcome questions as to my source of income. But enough to be a good son and show good intentions.

I dragged my attention back to the road as I-44 made a sharp curve south past Will Rodgers Park and the local satellite campus for Oklahoma State University to where I would jump onto I-40, a straight shot west almost to Los Angeles. At this hour of night, there was minimal traffic even within city limits, so I pushed the speed limit a bit. My favorite Rick Ross album was blasting from the Nissan's CD player, and I rapped along while my mind wandered through the possibilities for this weekend's entertainment.

Ironically, I'd known little about the cargo I ferried east several times a month when I'd started this job. A dedicated athlete throughout my school days, I'd never touched anything that might impair my performance on the field. And since I'd been raised by a devoutly Christian mother and attended parochial Catholic schools, even the street lingo was unfamiliar to me. I listened to rap to keep me awake on the long cross-country drives, and I'd been stunned to realize how many of my favorite artists were rapping about what I was doing right now.

My all-time Rick Ross favorite, Push It to the Limit, could be about some hard-working trucker out on the road just trying to earn enough to support his family: "Port of Miami, port of my candy, ain't got nothing to lose . . . We suppotin' the family, never traffic for fun, only traffic for funds . . . I push and I push, I ride and I ride, tryin' to survive on 95 . . ."

But now I knew the lyrics actually described a delivery driver like me picking up a load of cocaine from Miami and transporting it up I-95. The Rick Ross remix Hustlin' with Jay-Z and Young Jeeezy was another of my favorites since I'd always seen myself as a natural-born hustler:

"Everyday I'm hustlin', hustle, hustlin' hustlin' . . . It ain't no coincidence that my age is a kilo . . . I stack all faces, squares white as pillowcases . . . Feds on my tail . . .Sheet mix, remix still talkin' white bricks . . . Two million records sold . . . Ya want them pretty things, I'm the one ya need to ask. They come cross the border, I'm fulfillin' ya order . . ."

I now knew those white bricks being hustled were kilo-sized blocks of cocaine smuggled across the border to be remixed into smaller "squares" for street sale. And like that hustler, I had some worries about feds on my tail but not enough to quit until I'd made a million or two of my own.

That said, I wasn't so stupid as to fry my brain with the stuff I drove. I believed in being "always the hustler, never the customer." As for those who did, no one was forcing them so it was easy to convince myself I wasn't doing anything really immoral. I wasn't robbing a convenience store or bank. I wasn't hurting anyone. I was simply providing a delivery service. A technically illegal and extremely well-paying delivery service, but a victimless one at worse.

Though one thing had changed on this trip. For the first time, I'd been invited to stay the night after delivering my load instead of staying at a hotel. The interior of the upscale condo house had been like a freaking movie. Bundles of money stacked high on tables. Girls in panties and bras separating out cash into ones, fives, tens, twenties, fifties, hundreds. Guys strolling around with guns in their shoulder holsters. Another room stacked high with kilo bricks of cocaine.

That they'd brought me inside signaled to me I'd finally earned their trust. Which meant maybe I could move up from just being a delivery boy. Take on some real responsibilities. Make some real money. Reach millionaire status. Yeah, I was feeling good!

Once past the turnoff to the OCU satellite campus, I swerved right onto the exit that would take me west toward LA. I quickly downshifted as the speed limit dropped from seventy-five to sixty, then to forty. My mission orders included taking seriously any speed limits or other local traffic ordinances along my route. Which was fine by me since I wanted to avoid police attention as much as my employers did, at least until I handed off the 350Z.

I slowed even further as I merged onto Highway 270, which would become Interstate 40 west of Oklahoma. But not soon enough, it would seem. In my rearview mirror, an Oklahoma Highway Patrol cruiser nudged its coal-black nose out of a patch of bushes. Then another.

> "Instant gratification can all be taken away just as instantly." —Abe Cruz

I let out a few curses as the two cruisers bumped onto the highway and settled in behind me. Neither turned on their lights or siren, so I kept driving, careful to stay just a mile or two under the speed limit. The highway here led through the industrial district with all kinds of furniture outlets and warehouses that were dark at this time of night except for the floodlights in their parking lots.

Five minutes went by with the highway patrol cruisers still at my bumper. Maybe they were just running my out-of-state plates. If so, the car would come back clean, and out-of-state plates were hardly unusual with the OCU campus right up the road and the much bigger Oklahoma University just a half-hour further south. I began to relax. A few more minutes and I'd be outside city limits and back to Interstate speeds.

But just as I let down my guard, red and blue lights began flashing in my rear-view mirror, and a brief whop-whop of the siren ordered me to pull over. I still wasn't worried as I obeyed. After all, I had a good cover story. When a trooper stepped out of the cruiser behind me and approached the driver's side of my vehicle, I quickly rolled down my window.

The trooper leaned in, an unsmiling gaze taking in my age and casual dress of tank top, shorts, and sandal. Keeping both hands on the steering wheel, I plastered on a smile and asked respectfully, "Is there a problem, officer?"

He didn't answer my question but demanded with a heavy southern drawl, "Driver's license and insurance, please."

I handed him both. Glancing over them, he frowned at me. "So what are you doing out here this time of night, boy?"

I still wasn't worried as I repeated the lie that had been so effective on a previous stop. "Just over for the weekend from Cali to visit my girlfriend up at OSU. Heading home now."

Cali was slang for University of Southern California. But this officer didn't seem to be buying my college student act. His frown became a scowl. "Have you been drinking?"

"No, sir!" I responded even more respectfully.

Then he asked me straight out, "Are there drugs or weapons in this car?"

"No, sir," I said emphatically, thankful this was in fact the truth.

"Stay right here." The officer walked back to his car, taking my driver's license and registration with him. I settled patiently to wait, expecting to be on the road again once he checked my documentation. But no more than sixty seconds later, two big, black SUVs pulled up. The men who climbed out wore civilian clothing, but their black windbreakers had large, white letters on the back. DEA for Drug Enforcement Agency. And they had dogs with them!

I was stunned. More than that, I was starting to panic. There was no way the DEA had just happened along at this hour of the night. Nor could they have responded this fast to a call from those two cruisers. Not unless they'd been expecting it. Expecting me!

My mind and heartbeat raced as I frantically tried to think. Had the condo where I'd made my delivery been under surveillance by counter-narcotics? If so, then they'd have the 350Z on video coming and going. Maybe those two cruisers hadn't been an ordinary speed trap. Was it possible I'd been tracked all the way from Ohio? For the first time, I recognized this could be serious.

Walking over to my window, a DEA agent repeated the trooper's earlier questions. "What are you doing here? What's in the car?"

Though scared, I kept my cool, answering respectfully and calmly. But the agent's expression made clear he thought I was lying. "Then you won't mind if we check the car."

The agent gestured to the dog handlers, who approached. Then he turned back to me. "Get out of the car."

I climbed out. The dogs were now circling the Nissan with their handlers. Another agent opened the trunk while others rummaged inside the vehicle. Though worried, I got my panic under control, confident the dogs wouldn't smell anything since there were no longer drugs in the car. As for the hidden compartments, even I couldn't spot them, and I knew they were there.

But though the dogs were still showing no reaction, one handler suddenly spoke up. "I smell Bondo!"

I didn't know then what he was talking about, but I learned later that Bondo is a fast-drying epoxy-based automotive repair putty. Nothing illegal, but to the DEA it raised red flags as it was routinely used to seal off hidden compartments, followed by a quick sanding and paint touch-up. The smell of fresh Bondo on a car was as telltale to a counter-narcotics agent as the scent of cocaine to a drug dog.

The first agent swung around on me. "Abraham Cruz, you're under arrest."

That's when I knew I was in real trouble. I dropped my head, making no effort to talk my way out of this, while one agent read me my rights and another slapped handcuffs on my wrists. I was then escorted up the embankment to the top of a small rise, where I was left in the custody of a highway patrol trooper.

More DEA agents swarmed around the silver Nissan. The dogs still weren't reacting, and it didn't look to me as though the agents had found anything. But that didn't make me feel better since if they really tore the car apart, there was no way they wouldn't find the money. I was busted, and I knew it. The only question was how much trouble I was in.

"We've got a hit!" I heard someone announce down below.

"Looks like they found something," the trooper standing beside me commented. He looked over at me, and I was surprised to hear a note of compassion in his voice as he asked quietly, "Son, what have you gotten yourself into?"

"I'm so sorry! I'm so sorry!" I didn't even lift my head as I babbled an apology to the trooper. I was in complete shock. After eighteen months of success, I just couldn't believe this was happening. "I don't know how I got into this!"

But that wasn't true. I knew exactly how I'd gotten into this. The choices that had led to this moment. If this were just a few years earlier, I'd have been begging God for help right now. But at this moment the thought didn't even cross my mind. It seemed way too late for prayer.

Running? Now that was an option to consider!

CHAPTER TWO
NOT GOOD ENOUGH TO STAY

MY FATHER LEFT WHEN I WAS FOUR years old. Why is a question I've asked myself since I was a kid. Did he feel he was too good to stay with my mom, brother, sister, and me? With more than thirty years now to think about it, my heart tells me it wasn't that we weren't good enough. Providing for a family is hard. When someone is weak and lacks the mindset of a champion, leaving is the easy way out. So maybe he felt he wasn't strong enough or good enough to stay and raise a family.

Thankfully, GOD is there for the fatherless, and looking back now I can see how many decent, caring, honorable father figures GOD has brought into my life over the years. I don't think I'd be alive and living free today without them, as you'll see.

I was born the summer of 1981 at White Memorial Hospital in east LA. My father was from Havana, Cuba. I never learned how he made it to the United States, but by the time I came along he was a commercial truck driver. Of Italian-Basque heritage, my mom had grown up in a small town in Sonora, Mexico, just south of Arizona. She'd moved to the United States with her husband, who was an American citizen. They had one daughter, my half-sister, who was ten years old when I was born.

I don't know when that marriage broke up or how Mom met my father. But my earliest memories are of living a normal family life in a decent house in a nicer area of southern Pasadena. My father's steady job as a truck driver allowed Mom to stay home with me and my brother David, born just eighteen months after me. My parents took us on Sundays to a Spanish-speaking church, where my father served as a deacon.

I have just a few memories of those days, and maybe they are more from seeing old photos than real memories. But I do remember my father taking David and me to the zoo where I got to ride an elephant. I remember him dropping a quarter into a child-sized mechanical race-car outside our neighborhood grocery store so I could pretend to be a race-car driver.

I have one vivid memory of my father lifting me up into the cab of his enormous eighteen-wheeler—and of Mom arguing angrily over him taking me out on the road at my age. In truth, all other memories I have of my parents together involve arguing. In fact, my very last memory of my father was him slamming his fist into a wall mirror in a fit of rage while Mom screamed for someone to call the police and I cowered away from the fighting and shattered glass under the couch.

So when my father disappeared from our lives, I didn't really miss him as a person. I never knew him well enough to miss him—or to notice that this time when he drove away in his big truck, he never came back. What I did miss as I grew up and came to understand that we were now a single-parent household was the idea of having a father. Not my father specifically but any father.

And what I did notice was how his leaving affected our family. I have many sad memories of Mom crying. Without my father's income, she could no longer afford to stay in our comfortable middle-class home, so we were forced to move. Pasadena was basically split east-west by the Ventura Freeway, or Highway 210, a massive snarl of four and eight lane roads, exchanges, and overpasses. South of 210 was the more affluent section of Pasadena. North Pasadena was what the government called "the projects" and Hollywood liked to describe as "the hood."

Mom moved us into a one-bedroom apartment there, all she could afford. She put a bunkbed in the one bedroom for David and me while my mom and sister slept on blow-up mattresses in the living-room. That was our basic living arrangement all the way through my teen years. My sister soon moved out on her own, but it was typical of Mom to give David and me the only bedroom. She always sacrificed herself for her family.

The apartment had cockroaches, no matter how much bug-spray we used. We found roaches in our bed, crawling through our clothing, even in the food. I remember picking roaches out of my cereal bowl, then eating the cereal because we couldn't afford to throw food away. When your stomach hurts bad enough from hunger, believe me, you'll eat whatever is in front of you just to survive!

> "Every situation in life molds us and prepares us for the next challenge." —Abe Cruz

The neighborhood itself was run-down with bars on windows and doors, graffiti all over the walls, trash all over the streets, barbed wire, broken sidewalks, and potholes. Gang-bangers and drug-dealers loitered on corners so that David and I were scared to explore around outside, especially after dark. It's funny, since I know the climate is basically the same all over LA, but my memories at our first home in southern Pasadena are of sunny, blue skies while I remember the weather in North Pasadena as always dark, gloomy, and sad.

After my father left us, Mom went to the church we attended to let the leaders know what had happened. After all, Dad had been a deacon there. Not one church leader offered any help, spiritually or financially. Was this because they took my father's side as man of the house? Or somehow blamed my mother for not holding onto her husband?

More questions for which I never got an answer. Since the rest of her family was back in Mexico, Mom had no one else she could call on. Life from then on became a matter of daily survival.

For a while, Mom got food stamps and other social services. She took on two and three jobs at a time, everything from cleaning houses to office jobs. She took night classes and gradually worked her way up to secretarial work. My father never sent any child support, and in fact, I never saw him again to this day.

Looking back, I can't imagine how lost Mom must have felt with three kids to take care of on her own with no money. But she always stayed strong. She always kept a smile on her face. She was deeply hurt that the church leaders who'd been my father's comrades as deacon did nothing to help us, and once we moved to our new apartment, she stopped taking us to church. But she never lost her faith in GOD or stopped encouraging us to be thankful.

"*Cuenten sus bendiciones, m'ijos* [count your blessings, my sons]," she'd say. "*Dios está con nosotros* [GOD is with us]. He won't let us down."

Giving thanks to GOD became an ingrained part of my daily schedule. When we woke up, we thanked GOD for giving us one more day. Before we ate, we thanked GOD for the food. Sometimes that wasn't much. I can remember making meals for my brother and me while Mom was at work that were just butter on bread or a tortilla because that's all we had. But it was healthy food that filled our stomachs, which not everyone has, and we still thanked GOD for that. Before going to bed, we thanked GOD again for bringing us through another day.

As a child, I admit I did see the poverty when I looked around our neighborhood and the way we lived, especially in comparison to other more fortunate kids I saw. But today I count it one more blessing to have grown up the way I did. At a very young age, I developed basic survival instincts. I learned resiliency and how to adapt to new environments. When I was older and began reading books on leadership, I discovered that adaptability and resiliency are key assets for success. Every situation in life molds us and prepares us for the next challenge. That includes poverty and hard times.

By those standards, my mom has been an incredible success as well as an incredible person. No matter what the situation, you stay strong, you stay positive, and you forever keep your faith. That's always been Mom's philosophy for success.

Mom also told us that as long as we stuck together as a family, we'd be fine. Our love for each other was all we needed to get us through. There were people out there who'd never had the opportunity to love, she'd remind us. She assured us she'd never leave like our father did and that she'd help David and me become strong young men.

And Mom kept those promises. Even when I hit rock-bottom, I never doubted she was there for me. And the principles she ingrained into her kids are what eventually turned me around and back out. She has been my model of what it means to have the mindset of champions. *Gracias* [thank you], Mom!

But if you'd asked me back when we were living in the hood what it meant to be a champion, I'd have given a very different answer. A champion was someone who delivered win after win.

And in my world that someone was hands-down me!

CHAPTER THREE
BIG BROTHER

I WAS EIGHT YEARS OLD WHEN THE FIRST surrogate father figure who would shape my life introduced me to what would prove my ticket to the winner's circle—competitive sports. Mom was responsible for that too. Concerned that David and I had no real male role models, she enrolled us both in the Big Brother program.

Big Brothers (and Big Sisters for girls) is a community mentoring program that pairs children from low-income, single-parent homes with an adult volunteer who agrees to spend several hours a month with their appointed "sibling." I was quickly paired with a Big Brother named Ken Mendoza.

Ken was the sparkplug that kickstarted my passion for sports. More importantly, he showed me what a loving, kind, compassionate father could be. In truth, I have far more memories of spending great days with Ken than with my own father. Though the Big Brother program required meeting with me only twice a month, Ken began picking me up most weekends. He took me to the Pasadena Athletic Club, where he showed me how to swim and properly shoot a basketball. He gave me my first taste of lifting weights. He took me out for pizza.

My younger brother David still hadn't been paired with his own Big Brother, so it wasn't long before Ken invited him along as well. Ken and his wife Rose were both UCLA grads and big fans of the Bruins, UCLA's football team. They took David and me to the Rose Bowl for our first football game. They took us to nice restaurants where we learned formal table manners. They invited us to their home for holidays and other special occasions.

For the first time in my memory, I was being exposed to a far more upscale world than the drugs, gangs, dirt, poverty, and cockroaches of our neighborhood. The contrast to our own lives couldn't be starker. By this age, I'd grown into a very shy child. Part of this was because David and I had now graduated from being afraid to walk our neighborhood's unsafe streets to attending an elementary school not much safer. I saw first and second graders carrying switch-blades. The school was ninety percent minorities and low-income enough that three-fourths of the student body qualified for free lunches. I'm sure the teachers tried, but with kids crammed thirty to forty in a classroom, the education we received was marginal.

Outside on the playground, there was minimal supervision or protection against bullies. Even in that low-income neighborhood, David and I stood out as poor, our thrift-store clothing ragged and not always clean. I only had a few outfits so I'd wear the same shirt or pants two or three times a week, something my classmates were quick to jump on.

My beat-up shoes were even worse. We couldn't afford to replace my Payless sneakers when they wore holes in the soles—or buy more durable name brands. To play sports, I would wear multiple layers of socks, sometimes five or six pairs, which in turn made my feet hot and sweaty. When kids teased, I'd tell them it was my style. In reality, it was to protect my toes and soles from getting cut up.

In truth, the clothing and shoes weren't such a big deal to me. I understood Mom was raising us by herself while other kids had both mom and dad. Being poor was just our reality. Hitting early puberty was another matter. I began growing so quickly that by age ten I was 5'5". As an adult, I topped out at 5'9", on the short side for an athlete. But in later elementary, I was one of the biggest, strongest kids for my age.

That wasn't so bad, but the raging hormones responsible for early growth left me with terrible acne. I had breakouts all over my face, chest, back, shoulders and neck. The other kids started calling me "crater face" and "pizza face." I could brush off all the mocking about my clothes and shoes, but not what kids were saying about my appearance. I felt so ugly I couldn't even look at myself in the mirror.

Athletics became my escape. Whatever sport Ken took David and me to see—basketball, football, swimming, wrestling—he would spend hours showing us how to make the same moves. He played catch with us, practiced hoops, taught us to run football plays. Everything I learned from Ken and watching pro sports, I would take out onto the playground at recess. Pretty soon kids two and three years older were letting me join their football games. At least out there I was good enough that no one made fun of me.

> "Going through trials is what builds endurance, perseverance, and strength of character."
>
> —Abe Cruz

Beyond the Mendozas, I have two great memories of those years. The first was my older sister. Though she no longer lived at home, she'd visit from time to time, taking David and me out for fried chicken or to the beach.

My other great memory was TGIF—Thank GOD It's Friday. Now that David and I were a bit older, Mom had started dating or going out with friends on Friday nights. My brother and I would sit in front of the TV eating Little Caesar's pizza or Japanese takeout. That's when I created my first fitness program, doing push-ups, sit-ups, calf-raises, and other exercises during the commercials. I soon noticed the increase in my muscle development.

I couldn't blame Mom for wanting to get away from us occasionally. For all the good times with Ken and Rose, I wasn't an easy kid to deal with. Despite being shy and easily embarrassed, I was already showing the aggressive streak that would help me succeed in sports, especially if I felt people were trying to push me around.

I was basically two different kids. Mom had taught me to show respect, be considerate of others, and address adults appropriately. "Yes, sir. No, sir. Yes, ma'am. No ma'am. Thank you." That's the kid I was around the Mendozas.

But at school and the after-school program David and I attended until Mom got off work, I'd started getting into a lot of fights and other disciplinary problems. When other kids teased me over my clothes and acne, I no longer just walked away but would lash out verbally and with my fists. I even picked up tables and threw them. I got suspended a couple of times and was eventually reassigned to an alternative school.

Also, I didn't mind obeying rules if they made sense to me. If they didn't, I started what would become a long-term pattern of arguing back or simply ignoring rules I felt didn't apply to me. That included at home with my mom. I was constantly talking back to Mom. David was no angel either. I'm sure we scared off any guy who tried to date my mom.

Mom, we're really sorry about that, but thank you!

Typically, the Big Brother commitment is for a year. Ken and Rose remained active in our lives for at least three to four years. Committed Christians, they began taking David and me to church Sunday mornings if we stayed over Saturday night. I'll admit I went to church only to please Ken and Rose. I still said my prayers and took for granted there was a GOD, but I didn't think about it much otherwise. I was too focused on my own problems and life.

In contrast, Mom talked all the time about faith. "Don't worry, *m'ijos* [sons]" she would assure us. "Even if your father isn't here, *Jehová nos va a proveer* [Jehovah will provide for us]. Everything's going to be okay."

My father hadn't so much as called since he walked out, and by this time I'd stopped expecting him to return. But one day about five years after he'd left, something unusual did happen. Mom had picked David and me up from school. We were approaching our apartment building when we spotted a car parked outside.

Mom drove right on past our building. We ended up spending a few nights with friends before she'd let us go back to the apartment. She told us later that the car belonged to my father, who had come to kidnap us from her custody. That was our last contact of any sort with him. Much later, Mom told us he'd moved to Miami, remarried, and had another family.

Two good things happened when I was ten. Mom's finances improved enough to move us out of the "hood." Though still a one-bedroom apartment and still north of Hwy 210, it was a much nicer area. My memories are of once again seeing bright, blue skies. We did still have a few roaches but not nearly as bad.

The other good thing was being enrolled for the first time in competitive sports. Thanks to Ken, David and I had both become outstanding athletes for our age. By age ten, it was rare to see me without a basketball or football, and I spent my time outside of school practicing any chance I got. The alternative school where I'd been enrolled after our move was across the street from Victory Park, home to the local Pop Warner program, a non-profit Little League that included football for boys and girls ages 6-14 along with cheerleading.

Teams were organized according to height and weight as well as age. With my growth spurt, I wasn't yet eleven years old when I found myself on a team called the Pasadena Panthers with kids who were twelve and thirteen. Thanks to Ken's training, I was not only advanced athletically but physically fit and fast. I also had a drive to win for which I can thank Mom, who not only pushed herself but her sons to have a strong work ethic.

"If you're going out there, give it all you've got," Mom would tell us. "If you're not going to give it your all, then don't bother doing it!"

The Pasadena Panthers head coach had a similar philosophy. Coach Pitts taught us that if we wanted to win, there was no other option but hard work. He started me at wide receiver and defensive end. We went 14-0 that season, and by the end I'd earned the nickname "Hands" because I could catch any ball thrown my direction.

Around this time, Ken and Rose had their first child, so they couldn't spend as much time with David and me. But Ken did make a few of my games. In one game, I made an over-the-shoulder catch that resulted in us winning the game. That catch was something he'd taught me, so having him there to see it was a special blessing.

I can't give enough thanks for the Big Brothers program and all the volunteers who pour their lives into kids like me. If it wasn't for Ken, I'm not sure where I'd have ended up. Maybe on the streets peddling drugs with a gang like so many other kids of my neighborhood.

CHAPTER FOUR
BIRTHING A MINDSET

AFTER FOOTBALL SEASON ENDED, I moved straight into basketball, another sport in which Ken had spent a lot of time drilling David and me. The basketball program was held at the Boys and Girls Club, a volunteer organization that provides after-school and summer programs in sports, tutoring, life skills, arts, and other activities for millions of American children, mostly low-income.

The Pasadena club had a basketball gym, pool tables, video games, and a lot of other fun activities. But it was a full hour's walk from our school, and with my shabby clothes and acne, I was embarrassed to be around other kids, especially girls. Now pushing 5'6", I was starting to notice the opposite gender, but I was extremely self-conscious at how skinny, awkward, and ugly I must look to them.

Still, I really wanted to play basketball so I'd walk the hour there and back. Once again, I was advanced enough for my age that I was bumped to an older team where my teammates were all thirteen and fourteen. While we didn't win the championship that year, I was nominated runner-up for MVP (Most Valuable Player). David was also playing football and basketball, though on younger teams, and the Cruz brothers were gaining a name as up-and-coming athletes.

I was also learning my first real lessons in becoming a team player as well as the discipline and skill needed to be a top athlete. To be honest, my coach drove me crazy, and I know I drove him crazy too. Playing against Ken, I'd learned I had natural athleticism and could dribble circles around most other players. Full of energy,

I just wanted to grab the ball and sink a basket, preferably a three-pointer. But the coach insisted we learn the fundamentals. He'd call out a play and expect us to execute it. Now, of course, I know his style of coaching was preparation for higher levels of basketball and that he was teaching me patience and discipline without me even realizing it. Overall, he was another great role model in my childhood.

That same summer of 1992, I was introduced to another hero—basketball Hall of Famer Michael Jordan. He'd led his team to victory and was named MVP two years in a row. We didn't have internet back then, so I'd avidly watch every game and listen to his interviews. I found out that the greatest player of all time had been cut from the team his freshman year of high school. How did he bounce back? By work ethic, drive, passion, and sacrifice.

After watching his games, I'd practice Jordan's moves over and over for hours. With enough repetition, I was able to do them. Not like Michael Jordan but pretty good for an eleven-year-old. The famous one-arm take-off from the free-throw line. Switching to the left hand. Making six three-pointers in one half of play. I did all of these in games over the next few years.

But what I learned from Michael Jordan went way beyond basketball. It was about having the mindset of a champion. The idea that I could be successful at anything if I focused hard enough on it. At that age, I thought only in terms of sports. I eventually came to understand I could apply that same mindset to become successful at anything else I wanted. Bottom line, mindset, heart, and work ethic are the solutions to challenges and obstacles in life.

My second year in football and basketball was just as successful. Now eleven, I was again playing with kids two and three years older. I wasn't the biggest kid, but I was fast and so aggressive that my nickname "Hands" was upgraded to "Animal." In basketball we finished the season fifteen-zero and won the league championship.

Playing basketball. Playing football. Practicing. Training. I didn't really know what it was all about, but I loved the feeling of winning. I loved the feeling of accomplishment. The feeling of overcoming obstacles. Ken had started it all when he introduced me to sports. But then something inside of me took over and loved the competition. Focus on winning. That was the mindset I developed at an early age. Life was a constant battle with unending challenges, and it was up to me to fight hard enough to overcome those challenges.

One reason winning in sports became such a focus was because the rest of my life wasn't going so going well. The alternative school was designed to give second chances to kids who'd had behavioral and academic issues in regular school. That meant a lot of disciplinary problems. And unlike my prior school, these students weren't necessarily from low-income families but were often there for general bad behavior. A lot of them had money. They wore brand-name shoes and clothing, real gold chains, earrings. Kids like me were dirt beneath their feet. I started getting into fights again when they would bully me.

> "Mindset, heart, and work ethic are the solution to life's challenges." —Abe Cruz

Since I'd gotten used to playing with much older kids, I began cutting classes to hang around with other truants across the street at the park, some of them already in high school. They'd be smoking and doing drugs while we shot baskets. Thankfully, I was too into sports to compromise my skills that way. But to fit in, I started shop-lifting, trying to look cool with big, baggy pants, boxers hanging out, and an earring. I lied to my mom that friends had given me the clothing. I was now constantly fighting with her as she hated the hip-hop look and wanted me to dress clean-cut.

By seventh grade, my acne was so bad I couldn't stand making eye contact with people. I knew by their expressions that all they saw were the scars and scabs that made me look like some old-time small-pox victim. I'd see a group of cute girls glancing my way and was sure they were laughing at me. In despair, I asked Mom what I'd done to get such bad acne. Was GOD punishing me? If so, why?

"I'm sorry to say you inherited it from me," Mom responded. "I've always had a problem, but I eventually grew out of it, and you will too."

That didn't make me feel any better about looking like a monster now. I found some medicine called Retin-A Mom was taking for adult acne and plastered it all over my face, hoping that might help. I didn't know you weren't supposed to go out in the sun while using Retin-A. My face turned bright red, then black and peeling like I was some kind of zombie. I became so depressed and self-conscious I simply stopped going to school.

There was a park just north of the Boys and Girls Club. I'd tell Mom I was heading to school, then walk the hour to the park. There I'd spend the day inventing my own fitness routines, then working on basketball and football skills until it was time to head to the club for basketball practice. By the end of seventh grade, I'd missed over ninety percent of the school year.

Those were tough years, not just for me but my entire family. It couldn't have been easy for Mom working such long hours and coming home to rebellious, unhappy sons who were constantly talking back. But looking back, I wouldn't change anything because going through those times is what molded us to be who we are today as a family. Going through trials is what builds endurance, perseverance, and strength of character. That's in the Bible too.

So don't pray asking God, "Why me, heavenly Father? Why are you putting me through this?" Just figure it out and keep moving forward. That's something else I learned from Mom.

And thank God for sports. In all the sadness, sports was my escape from reality and the only place I didn't feel a loser. Working out every day at the park, running drills, practicing my shots, I could see I was getting better daily. Though I basically lost the school year, I had another great season of football and basketball. And thanks to those, I met a man who would influence and mold me for the better over the next eight years and to the present day.

CHAPTER FIVE
NEW BLESSINGS

A CAL STATE GRADUATE, OSCAR CEPEIDA had a legal practice in Alhambra, an affluent neighborhood south of Pasadena. He loved GOD, loved kids, loved sports, and loved giving back to the community. He'd gotten involved in coaching because he had four kids of his own, all of whom played on various teams. When I met him, he was coaching an AAU (Amateur Athletic Union) traveling basketball team named Alhambra Magic.

One of the largest volunteer sports organizations in the world, the AAU has been training champions for more than a hundred and thirty years with three-quarters of a million players and a hundred-fifty-thousand volunteers just in the United States. Oscar was always looking for new talent for his team. The director of the Pasadena Boys and Girls Club told him he had a kid who was the best eleven-year-old player he'd seen. Oscar came down to watch me play. After the game, he approached and invited me to play on his team.

I can't imagine what I must have looked like to Oscar when I showed up for my first practice over at Alhambra High School. I was wearing a pair of well-worn green short overalls over a University of Las Vegas T-shirt and a hoop earring in my left ear. My Payless sneakers had huge holes in the bottom, so I had on boots over multiple socks.

My new teammates all had on proper basketball shoes—Nike and Reeboks. I was already self-conscious and thinking these kids were going to be like all the others, teasing me for my shoes and clothing. But that never happened, and I could see immediately it was because of Oscar. It wasn't that he told them not to tease me.

He didn't have to because he was a real leader, a true example for his players of what it meant to be a good person. He demanded the best out of us because he gave us the best out of him. Knowing him as I do now, Oscar wanted the best for people, period!

From my first practice with Alhambra Magic, I was hooked. Oscar's energy and love for the game came across in every practice. He made us better daily. But he also really showed concern for his players. He made me feel that he cared about me like a father would. I also saw very quickly that Oscar had a deep faith in GOD. He would always pray with us before practices and games.

"Put GOD first, pray, respect GOD," he would tell us, "and GOD will take care of you."

But though I loved my new team and coach, getting over to Alhambra for practice wasn't easy. It was too far to walk there and back as I'd done to the Boys and Girls Club, and since we often practiced well into the evening, I couldn't expect Mom to keep driving all the way down there to pick me up.

Thankfully, it wasn't long before Oscar started offering to drive me home. His vehicle was a Suburban big enough to squeeze the whole team in when necessary. Once he'd dropped off anyone else he was taking home, I'd sit up front with him for the drive to Pasadena. I was embarrassed to put my coach to so much trouble but also grateful since the only other option was not practicing or quitting the team altogether. He'd often stop at a Seven-Eleven to buy each of us a cold drink. Then we'd talk about my life and family. I was soon opening up to him, including about my father leaving.

"Look, Abe, you're a good kid," Oscar told me. "You just need some direction. I'm here to help you become a successful young man. But if you want to keep playing for me, I've got some rules you're going to have to follow. First, you must respect and love your mother. Second, you have to get rid of that earring."

He said this in a nice way. I wasn't happy about it, but I knew what he meant. Coach Oscar expected his players to look clean-cut and respectable. He'd already made clear his opinion of pants drooping below the butt and other such styles.

"And third," he finished, "you have to keep up your grades."

By now there was nothing I wouldn't have done to keep playing for Coach Oscar. But how could I tell him I'd skipped most of the last year of school and would unquestionably be failing seventh grade? I felt absolutely horrible, sad, and embarrassed all at once. I was sure he'd throw me off the team if he found out. I'd just have to hope he didn't!

From that point on, Oscar became a very special father figure in my life all the way to the present day. Ken had been that for me and David over the past four years, and I'd never forget all he'd been and done in my life. But he and Rose were now raising their own young family, and understandably our Big Brother relationship had to phase to something different.

But as I've witnessed throughout my entire life, GOD never abandons you. He puts you through intensive training in preparation for your future, and when he's finished with one stage of training, he moves you on to the next. But he will also send you a new blessing. Ken was a very big blessing GOD sent at a very difficult time in my life. Oscar and his entire family were a new blessing.

For the rest of that school year and summer, I continued to practice with Alhambra Magic. Pretty soon I was traveling to tournaments all over the region. That alone was an incredible experience as I'd never been outside East LA. Nor did I have to worry anymore about holes in my shoes or ragged clothing as the team provided uniforms and Oscar purchased me a pair of brand-new basketball shoes. That year at age twelve, I was named by the premier basketball magazine *Slam* as one of the top three point guards for my play bracket in the entire country.

Gradually over the months, I opened up more to Oscar. My seventh grade year was almost over when I admitted I wasn't going to school. Of course he wanted to know why. I was scared to tell him. I was sure he'd be angry. Sure he'd throw me off the team. But I finally poured out how much I hated the alternative school, how miserable and embarrassed I was with the kids mocking my torn-up shoes, clothing, and horrible acne. I didn't even feel safe going there anymore with all the fights I was getting into.

> "God puts you through intensive training in preparation for your future." —Abe Cruz

When I finished, I waited for Oscar to yell at me as I deserved. Instead of getting mad or judging, what he did next was something I never expected. He asked if I'd be interested in attending the school his own children attended, All Souls, a multi-language private TK-8th grade Catholic school in Alhambra.

I was speechless. I didn't even know how to respond. I finally said, "I don't know. But maybe we can talk to my mom."

I was really excited as we headed home after practice to talk to my mom. I knew nothing about this school, and I didn't really know Oscar and his family that well. But I knew in my heart this would be an opportunity that could change my life. Besides, anything had to be better than where I was!

When Oscar parked outside my apartment building, we didn't go in right away. Instead we sat there in the front seat of his big, gray Suburban while he described what my life would be like at this new school.

"Your life will completely change, Abe. At All Souls you'll get an outstanding education that will prepare you for high school. You'll play football and basketball, and you'll win championships. You'll go onto a good high school, where you'll win more championships that will bring you to the attention of colleges. You'll get an athletic scholarship to college that will prepare you for the pros. You put God first, and God will bless you and open doors to give you a good future."

I didn't really understand everything Oscar was describing. But I believed his vision for my future, and I believed this was a door God was opening for me. I wish I could say I was thinking right then of putting God first and living my life for God. In truth, I was thinking only of fulfilling my dream to become a champion and winner like Michael Jordan. What I did consciously think was how I could give Mom a better future after all she'd sacrificed for her children.

Of course that would only happen if Mom said yes. Oscar and I finally headed inside to meet with my mom. Seated in our tiny living-room, Oscar started by explaining that I'd shared with him my problems at the alternative school and how I was failing seventh grade.

"I think I have a solution. I can get Abe and David both into All Souls Catholic School in Alhambra where my kids attend. It's a great school that would prepare your sons for a better future."

But the moment Oscar mentioned private schooling, Mom started shaking her head. "*No tengo dinero pa eso* [I don't have money for that]."

"*No te preocupas* [don't worry about that]," Oscar assured her. "All Souls has an excellent financial aid program. I know we can work something out. What's important is to get Abe out of the bad situation he's in. Perhaps you aren't aware of what a unique talent your son has. He has great potential as an athlete. A good education like All Souls could make a complete difference for his future."

Mom wasn't convinced. In truth, she knew nothing about my new world of sports. She was too busy working, sometimes going from her job at a doctor's office to another job at a bank to cleaning houses in her off-hours, to attend any of our games. So she had no idea whether I was any good or not. To her these programs were just something to keep David and me off the streets and out of trouble.

Nor did it make sense to her for a total stranger to be offering such an incredible opportunity out of the blue. There had to be a catch somewhere!

But to me it did make sense. After all, I'd seen and heard plenty about celebrities, especially pro athletes like Michael Jordan, getting special treatment. And why not? It wasn't a charitable handout. Those who got such treatment had to work their tails off and become the best they could be to earn those special privileges. It all came down to sacrifice and hard work. I was willing to put in that kind of work to go to All Souls, and I truly felt God was opening the door for me to a bigger future. I just had to convince my mom.

Mom kept raising objections. What about transportation? All Souls was even further from our neighborhood than Alhambra High School where Oscar coached our team. And there were far more expenses than tuition at a private school. There were uniforms, books, activity fees. Oscar kept reassuring her that these could all be arranged.

At last Mom said, "Thank you for this. But I can't make a decision immediately. Let me talk with my sons, and I'll get back to you."

Once Oscar left, Mom asked me two questions. "Tell me, *m'ijo*, do you trust this man? And do you really want to go to a brand-new school where you won't know anyone?"

"Yes. Mom, I do trust this man," I answered with no hesitation. "And I'll know a lot of people. The other kids on the team already go to All Souls, and I get along really well with all of them. Please, *please* let me go, Mom!"

I kept begging as I'd never begged for anything in my life. Mom finally cut me off. "All right, just leave me alone. Let me think. I'll let you know later tonight."

I wanted to keep pushing, but I also knew that if I didn't obey, she'd most likely just decide I couldn't go. So I dropped the subject. "Okay, Mom, *te amo*! [I love you!]"

Mom finally came back to me. "We need to pray about this that Father God will give us our answer and direction. In the morning I'll make my decision."

I couldn't argue with that. We knelt together. Mom prayed, "*Dios mío, Padre nuestro en los cielos* [Dear God, our Father in heaven]. Did you really send these people to help us? Please show us if this is the right move."

I went to sleep that night looking forward confidently to a bright future. Sure enough, when I woke up the next morning, Mom told me she'd decided this was God's will for us, an opportunity she'd never on her own be able to give us. "Go ahead and call Coach Oscar. Let him know it's a yes."

I was so excited I had to control myself to punch in Oscar's number. I was so ready for a new beginning! I was ready for more in life. *Thank you, thank you, Father God!*

CHAPTER SIX
A WAY OUT

As soon as I told Oscar it was a go, he went to work. I know he had to pull some strings to persuade the principal to let in this troubled kid from an alternative school who'd skipped most of seventh grade. Coach Oscar assured him I had potential and that my athletic abilities would help raise awareness for the school. He must have been convincing because that year David and I both transferred to All Souls.

With a summer birthday, I'd always been one of the youngest in my grade, so repeating the year turned out to be a very positive experience, allowing me to tackle academics as well as sports and other areas as one of the more mature students in my grade. Those two years at All Souls proved to be some of the best times of my life. Everything Oscar said I could expect pretty much happened just as he'd told me.

To begin with, Mom decided that if David and I were to make a fresh start at All Souls, we needed to move closer to our new world. Without funds, she couldn't immediately leave our current apartment or employment. Since I was spending so much time practicing and playing for Coach Oscar, I moved on ahead, living with Oscar's brother and his wife, whose two sons also attended All Souls. Oscar and his wife Ofelia had two daughters and two sons, one of whom was in David's grade. I also attended church with them, which was the one connected to All Souls school.

I'd never known a big, whole family like this with both parents in the home and aunts and uncles and cousins living close, and I loved being around them. They all seemed the most perfect family on earth. I'd also never lived in such beautiful, prosperous surroundings. Not just a big house in an upscale neighborhood and nice cars and all the other things our single-parent, low-income household could never afford. Since All Souls was a top-rated private school, the students were predominantly well-off with a living standard far beyond anything I'd ever seen before or dreamed. Once again, my eyes were being open to the possibilities of a very different world and future.

It wasn't long before Mom was able to move to Alhambra. Our new apartment had two bedrooms so she could finally move out of the living-room. There was even a community pool in the apartment complex. I was happy Mom, David, and I were together again. But I did miss the lifestyle I'd enjoyed with the Cepeidas as well as the big-family atmosphere. That would influence some later decisions—and not always in a good way!

Still, my new beginning was everything Oscar had assured me. I played my first season of flag football with the Catholic Youth Organization (CYO) of LA, the interscholastic sports program for more than one hundred-seventy Catholic elementary/middle schools throughout the Los Angeles area. I made a total of 107 touchdowns, and our team finished the season 38-0, winning the first championship in All Souls history. That same football season, I played tackle football for the East LA Bobcats, starting as a running back and wide receiver and ending as team quarterback.

Basketball season followed football. Since I played with Coach Oscar's traveling team and trained all year round, I was always in good basketball shape. I became known for wearing my strength shoes everywhere, even at school. These were training sneakers with a special platform at the front that put extra strain on your calf muscles, giving them a heavy workout that helped you run faster and jump higher. Wearing them all day as I did, I was the strongest, fastest kid on the All Souls Panthers, and I had my first dunk at age twelve.

I was also doing well academically and socially for the first time in my life. I'd earned the respect of both student body and faculty as an athlete. Since All Souls was a private school, we all wore the same uniform, so I didn't stand out for not having brand-name clothing. I still had problems with acne, but that too was improving. And I hadn't been in a single fight or other trouble since transferring to All Souls.

I wish I could say that was true elsewhere. I'd stopped shoplifting since the move to Alhambra. After all, my sports shoes, uniforms, and other school needs were all provided. But one day at the beginning of basketball season, I left home for a training run in my strength shoes. It was pouring down rain so I'd bundled up in my big, black CYO football championship jacket. I ran a good two miles to a CVS pharmacy, where I decided to treat myself to a mint-chocolate-chip ice-cream cone, my favorite flavor.

I only had one dollar, enough for the ice-cream cone. Then I spotted some wristbands, a flashy fashion statement that would be just the thing for my next basketball game. Since I didn't have enough money for ice cream and wristbands, I stuffed the wristbands into my jacket pocket. Paying for the ice cream, I headed out of the store, eating my cone and congratulating myself on how stealthily I'd managed my theft.

But I was barely out the door when a security guard came after me. My ice-cream cone fell splat to the ground as he hustled me back inside, where I was sternly informed that they'd caught my theft on camera. I couldn't argue it was someone else since my CYO jacket and strength shoes were pretty conspicuous. By now I was scared out of my wits. The guard made me wait in the back until my mom arrived.

Mom swiftly settled the matter—returning the wristbands, of course, and whatever else she had to do to keep me from being prosecuted. But as soon as we were outside, she grabbed me by the ear. Dragging me painfully to the car, she told me harshly, "If you ever steal anything again, I won't come and get you! I'll just leave you to the police!"

> "It's how you handle the losses that determines and molds you into your future."   —Abe Cruz

I knew she meant it too. Getting caught and seeing Mom that angry was a big enough scare I never did shop-lift again. For the next several months, I had extra chores to do as punishment. But though a major wakeup call, that call sadly didn't last forever.

I was just lucky Mom didn't bench me. That season, we had another incredible team. We reached the playoffs 15-0. In a semi-finals game, I sprained my ankle pretty bad, but we still won and headed to the next round against St. Eugene School, the only other undefeated team. No one thought I could play, but I'd seen athletes like Michael Jordan and Magic Johnson play through injuries, and I was determined to follow their example.

We iced my ankle well, then taped it up and added a brace. I was still in pain but sank almost thirty points, not quite enough to win. It was a disappointment, but my ankle soon healed, and we went on to win the next thirty-five games, finishing 50-1. The CYO championship was the rematch of the year—All Souls Panthers versus St. Eugene. We battled hard, but in the end they won, ending our season 50-2, both losses against the same team.

They'd earned it so we couldn't be too upset. Besides, there was always next year. I'd grown used to winning, but losing the championship gave me understanding and humility that life isn't always going to be a winning situation. It's how you handle the losses that determines and molds you into your future.

As soon as All Souls basketball season ended, I went straight into AAU travel ball. I was still playing for Alhambra Magic, but Oscar felt I was ready for an additional challenge, so he'd arranged for me to play as well for the 4-D All Stars, a team that traveled all over the United States to compete. The 4 Ds stood for Dedication, Determination, Desire, and Defense. That summer the 4-Ds had one of the best All Star teams for our age division, battling the top talent in the country and beating them all. It was an incredible experience, again showing me a whole different world out there to which I could aspire. By now I felt like a champion, and everyone around me agreed.

In the fall, I headed back to All Souls for my eighth grade year. Football season started with a 38-0 championship season to defend. Just like seventh grade year, we were unstoppable with an undefeated record all the way to the playoffs.

Then the unthinkable happened. I'd been having some trouble with Mom. She felt I was argumentative and disrespectful, which I'm sure was true. A typical teen, I'd complain about my chores and ask for money to buy things she didn't think I needed.

The playoffs were scheduled for the following Saturday. One evening that week, I was watching TV. I felt hot, so I opened a window to let in some fresh air. Mom didn't want the window open, probably because this was winter and the heat she was paying for was floating out that window. I know she asked me nicely more than once to shut the window. When I ignored her, she repeated more sternly, "Abe, I want that window closed."

Looking back now, I can't believe my response. Without lifting my gaze from the TV, I responded coolly, "Well, I want it open!"

Walking over to the window, Mom shut it with an audible thump. The moment she walked out of the room, I went over and opened the window again. When she came back and saw what I'd done, she was furious.

"You think you can just ignore me? You think you can disrespect me?" she said angrily. "Then fine! If you want to act like that, you're not playing your game this weekend."

Her words sent fear into my heart. Jumping up, I cried out, "What? You can't do that, Mom! I *have* to play!"

But she wouldn't budge. I burst into frantic pleading. "Please, Mom, I'm sorry! I'm sorry for disrespecting you. I'll do whatever you want. You can punish me any way you want after the game. But I have to play! You know what this means to me!"

"I accept your apology," Mom said calmly. "But you still can't play this weekend. All decisions have consequences in life, *m'ijo*. I gave you chance after chance to obey me, and you chose to defy me. You chose to disrespect me. So this is your punishment."

At fourteen, I was almost at my final adult height of 5'9", and with all my successes, I thought of myself as big, bad, and cool. But Mom brought me right back down to reality. It couldn't have been easy for her to maintain discipline over two sons now bigger, heavier, and stronger than her. But she was a strong woman herself and not about to let us walk all over her.

"I don't care how old you get," she told me firmly. "I'm your mother, and I will always be in charge."

To make things even more embarrassing, she made me call Oscar to explain why I wouldn't be able to help All Souls win their second championship on Saturday. I told him what had happened, hoping he'd intervene so I could play. Instead, he asked me, "Do you remember the three rules I said you'd have to follow if you want to play for me?"

"Yes, of course," I answered.

Oscar went on, "The most important of those rules is and always will be to respect your mother. Even if you disagree with her. It doesn't matter if she's right or wrong. That's your mother, and you must always respect her!"

Without hesitation, he added, "I'm on your mom's side. You'll come to the game and watch from the sidelines. But you won't play."

I was in shock and absolutely brokenhearted at Oscar's decision. When Saturday arrived, I remained on the sideline while my team ran out onto the field without me.

I'm such an idiot! I castigated myself. *Over a window I create this problem! All I had to do was close the dang window. But I couldn't do that! My own stubbornness did this to me!*

I sat there and watched as my team, the defending champions, was defeated. We'd broken all the school records—total touchdowns, undefeated season, first CYO championship, and everything else. Now our winning streak was over. I was too ashamed and embarrassed to even look at my teammates. I should have been out there to help my team. Instead, they'd all paid the price for my selfish, stupid act.

It was another hard lesson learned in life, and for me at fourteen, it was a major one. But when it was all over, I apologized again to my mom.

"Thank you for teaching me right from wrong," I told her, and I meant it. "*Te amo,* Mom. I love you!"

CHAPTER SEVEN
NOTHING COULD STOP ME BUT ME!

THANKFULLY, I DIDN'T HAVE TIME TO brood about my failure as we jumped into basketball practice the very next day. We'd gone 50-2 last season, coming in second to St. Eugene. This year we were determined to go all the way, and we did. For the second year in a row, All Souls and St. Eugene faced off for the championship. By the second quarter we had a big lead.

I still remember a couple big highlights of that game. First, I scored two back-to-back three-pointers from more than twenty feet. I had the ball again when the St. Eugene guard rushed out to contest. I could have shot it, but I pulled one of my Michael Jordan moves, faking the three-pointer, then a hard dribble to the left and straight to the hoop. I was just setting up for my "kiss the rim" pose when their tallest player stepped up to block me. In mid-air, I paused my shot, switched hands, and finished with a back-spin that dropped the ball right through the net.

To me this was no big deal, a move I'd done a hundred times in practice. But the entire gym erupted. St. Eugene battled hard to the end, but we won the championship, ending the year with a perfect 55-0. While it didn't make up for losing the football championship, it went a long way toward redemption.

Overall, I had two incredible years at All Souls and developed a lot of great friendships that have stuck with me through the good and bad, including my own mistakes and wrong choices, all the way to the present day. Everything Oscar assured me turned out to be true. Not once did I get teased or bullied at All Souls, and I sure saw the difference in getting a real education compared to my previous schools.

I also learned the truth of something another good friend, mentor, and successful businessman, Dr. Luis Arriaza, once told me. "Son, you can't save the world broke."

People usually think of this related to money—as in you need to make money to have it for helping others. And certainly a lot of successful entrepreneurs have invested their billions to fund world-saving endeavors. But being broke isn't just financial. It can refer to family, personal relationships, social and church networks, connections. You can't grow to your potential if you're broke when it comes to having great people in your life.

I might not have realized as a kid how rich I was. But looking back now, I know that having Ken Mendoza as my Big Brother, Coach Oscar taking David and me out of a bad situation, all the coaches and teachers who invested in me, and others along the way I haven't yet mentioned—that was all incredible wealth in the bank of my life. Not to mention community programs like Big Brothers, Pop Warner, Boys and Girls Club, AAU, and all the volunteers that make those possible.

That kind of riches others poured into me is what helped me survive rock-bottom and reach where I am today. It's why I feel so strongly about giving back to kids like I was and supporting these kinds of programs. It isn't just about sports. It's about making a difference. It's about saving lives.

> "You can't grow to your potential if you're broke when it comes to having great people in your life."
>
> —Abe Cruz

Going back to All Souls, since the school only went to eighth grade, I now had to decide where to attend high school. With Oscar's guidance, I ended up choosing St. Paul Catholic High School in southeast LA for several reasons. First, it had a top-ranked athletic program. St. Paul's football coach Marijon Ancich finished his career with the second-highest record of wins in California history and was known as the "dean" of high school coaches because so many of his players and assistants went on to become top pro athletes and coaches. St. Paul also had an excellent academic ranking with almost 100% of graduates going on to college, including on sports scholarships, which was my aspiration. An added bonus was that Oscar's daughter, who was two years older than me, attended there and was willing to provide transport.

At the beginning of my freshman year, Oscar reminded me, "Abe, you saw I was telling you the truth about All Souls and what you could achieve there. Now you're heading into high school. You need to focus and work hard because what happens there is going to determine your future. You're going to win more championships. You're going to be scouted for college and the pros."

This time I no longer had any doubts he was right, and I had every intention of working my tail off to continue winning. Even before the school year started, I began practicing with the freshman (junior varsity) football and basketball teams—both in the same day. It wasn't long before the varsity basketball coach invited me to practice with his team as well.

I put my heart and soul into practice. I wouldn't have managed if not for a great friend from All Souls whose family had moved a few blocks from St. Paul when he started attending there. They would feed me and let me rest up at their house after football practice before I headed back for basketball practice. If it got really late, they let me crash there overnight.

Of course with my All Souls track record, I didn't plan to start high school on JV. For three years I'd trained to play at the top, and I figured I was more than good enough to jump straight to varsity. Football season confirmed my self-confidence. The coaches started me on the JV freshman team as a wide receiver. I led the team with thirty-five touchdowns, and we won the league championship with a 16-0 season. I was voted best athlete on the JV team and moved up to varsity the week they started playoffs.

That didn't last long as the St. Paul Swordsmen were eliminated in the first round of the playoffs. By then I'd discovered that high school football, especially with a school of St. Paul's reputation, was a whole different class physically from All Souls. There were players almost a foot taller than me and twice my weight. Still, it was a great introduction of Abe Cruz, the celebrated All Souls' athlete, to my new student body.

Then basketball season started. I was excited when the coach told me, "All right, Abe, it's show time. You've made the varsity team. Now it's time to work!"

I had no issue with hard work and expected to have to prove myself. But once again I quickly found out that high school basketball was a whole different category than middle school. Where once I'd been tall for my age and position, at 5'9" I was now quite short for my team, most of the others ranging 6' to 6'7". That didn't bother me because my constant workouts had left me—in my opinion at least—the fastest and strongest on the court.

But it soon became clear my older teammates weren't happy about a freshman jumping the line. Most of the team were juniors and seniors, and they figured I should be paying my dues before getting court time. And it seemed the coach agreed because when the season opened, I sat on the bench while a senior played my starting spot of point guard.

I decided I'd just have to show them what I had. I started staying a couple extra hours after practice to lift weights and run drills. When I did get some play time, I knew I was bringing a fresh blast of energy to the court. But it didn't seem to matter how hard I worked. What good was it being a freshman on varsity if I never left the bench? At least if I'd stayed on JV, I'd be playing!

I knew we were facing a really tough league, and it was clear the coaches worried I'd be intimidated if they put a freshman out there. I also knew the coaches wouldn't appreciate hearing a freshman whining about playing time. So I bit my tongue, sat on the bench, and waited. But when our team hit a real losing streak and the coaches still weren't letting me play, I began questioning my decision to come to St. Paul.

The truth was that since I'd started playing sports, I'd never had to face a challenge like this. Oh, sure I'd lost a game here and there. But since I'd played my first Pop Warner football, I'd always been ranked among the best in my sport, and I'd accomplished pretty well anything I'd set myself to achieve. I'd come to take winning for granted, and I didn't appreciate being dumped back down to the bottom. Much less being on a losing team!

Then one day we lost another game. This time the coach hadn't let me play at all. By now I was ready to give up. On top of everything else, the academics here were demanding. I'd been assured St. Paul would be the door to a college sports scholarship. But if I couldn't even show what I could do on the court, what was the point of studying harder than I ever had in my life?

Why am I here? I kept asking myself. *If they won't let me win, why stay in this school?*

When I got home after the game, I gave Oscar a call. After pouring out all my complaints, I pleaded, "I'm not sure this was a good decision. Can I just leave? I don't think I can do this anymore."

"*Cálmate* [calm yourself], Abe," Oscar shushed me with his usual quiet composure. "I didn't lie to you before, did I? You had a great time at All Souls. And I'm not lying to you now. You're a freshman and the youngest on your team. It takes time, but if you just keep working and stay focused, you'll get there. Everything will work out for good, I promise. You just need to have patience and keep your faith. Now let's say a prayer together."

I'll be honest I didn't want to hear any of that at the time. I wanted instant gratification. But I've learned life isn't like that, and quick gratification can all be taken away from you just as instantly. I only wish I'd learned that lesson then. It would have saved me a lot of grief and heartache a few years down the line!

CHAPTER EIGHT
UP AND DOWN

I COULDN'T THINK OF ANYTHING ELSE TO do except become even fiercer and more aggressive at practice. Apparently, the coach liked my drive because he gave me more playing time in the next game. I still remember that game like it was yesterday. I played well, but it was the last two minutes of the game that changed the rest of the season for me. The score was tight. I made a steal and a three-pointer. Then in the last fifteen seconds, I faked a pass, made a quick crossover to the right, and landed a jump shot from the free throw line. I'd tied the score with thirteen seconds left on the clock. The entire gym went crazy.

We ended up losing on a free throw in the last few seconds, but that game showed the coaches and my older teammates I was more than capable of varsity play even as a freshman. The next game I started at point guard. I played most of the first half before the coach switched me out, then played most of the second half. We ended up winning our first league victory.

All right, Abe, you fought for this spot! I told myself. *Don't lose it!*

The next game was a wild card that would allow us to move on to the playoffs if we won. With just one win that season, we were the underdogs, and no one gave us a chance. I led the team in steals, and the next day I made the sports section of the Whittier Daily News as "the Freshman Sensation" and "the Thief of Bagdad."

For the rest of the playoffs, I was a starting point guard and led in steals every single game. To pretty well everyone's disbelief, we won the school's first-ever CIF (California Interscholastic

Federation) Division 4 championship. Only Oscar wasn't surprised. He'd predicted this after all.

"I knew you'd make it happen," he told me calmly.

From there we advanced to the state tournament where we again did the unexpected, winning all the way to the semi-finals. We lost by three points, but this was far beyond what the team had ever reached before, and we'd been playing against Baron Davis, one of the best high-school players in the country at that time who went on to a successful NBA career. So we were all proud of how we'd worked together to win games. The rest of my freshman year was great. After basketball season, I added track and varsity volleyball. I made the honor roll for the first time ever.

But I had no time to dwell on success. I went straight back into football training while still playing travel ball with the 4-D All Stars. Football was serious business at St. Paul with a living legend like Marijon Ancich as head coach. Coming off championships in freshman football and varsity basketball, I knew a lot more would be expected of me as a sophomore.

Then the unexpected happened. I was playing with my usual aggression when I smashed full-force into the tight end. He flew back, and one leg hit me straight in the crotch. Without going into gruesome detail, suffice it to say I was sidelined for the first half of the season, and the doctors weren't sure I'd ever be able to have kids (thankfully, they were wrong!). I finally did get to play my first varsity football game, but we didn't even make the playoffs.

Basketball wasn't much better. I started out with a great season but ended up hurting the same ankle I'd played on sprained against St. Eugene back in seventh grade. Our team didn't come close to repeating their championship win, and instead of going on to other sports, I spent the rest of that year and summer healing. In all it was a year of injury and a lot of chaos.

One thing I came away with from those years is that talent isn't enough. Some readers may say, "Sure, Abe, it's easy enough for you because you were born a natural athlete."

Okay, sure, your natural abilities are a big help. You should figure out what those are and go after them. But all the raw talent in the world won't get you anywhere without sacrifice, practice, and hard work. When I had extra time, I wasn't sitting on the couch playing video games and watching movies. I was out there putting in extra practice. Even as a ten-year-old on Friday nights, I was working out while watching TV.

And even when you do work your tail off and put all your heart into it, you won't always win. Sometimes the other guy is just better or luckier or part of a stronger team. Point is, when you get knocked down, go ahead and cry for a second. But then it's time to get back up, refocus, regroup, and get back to work!

> "All the raw talent in the world won't get you anywhere without sacrifice, practice, and hard work." —Abe Cruz

That's exactly what I did that summer after a disappointing sophomore year. I simply wouldn't allow anyone to outwork me. On top of training with the football and basketball teams, I put in more work each day, whether weight training, sprints, drills, or just studying Primetime football games and other footage to see where I could improve my performance.

I started my junior year stronger than ever, completely healed, and feeling this was my year to shine. With my injuries, no one had gotten to see what I could do last year, and that was going to change. I'd already won a CIF championship in basketball so I was determined to add one in football. This once-shy kid also had a new personality of confidence, self-esteem, and charisma.

At least that's how I saw it. My coaches had a slightly different perspective. As a Catholic school, St. Paul was known for emphasizing humility, hard work, and tradition—including on the sports field. Loud dress, personality, or attitude were not acceptable. Which didn't go well with my new personality. In my mind, I was ready to do everything St. Paul stood for, just cooler, louder, and flashier.

My coach quickly noticed I wasn't using the stance he'd taught us. Like my Pop Warner coach a few years earlier, he was systematically laying a foundation of fundamentals. But I saw my NFL heroes like Deion Sanders doing things a whole lot different, and I figured I was good enough to follow their lead instead of my coaches. It got to the point where my coach threatened not to start me if I couldn't follow the stance and techniques he'd laid out for us all. I wasn't about to lose playing time, so I knuckled under.

My standout attitude showed in my dress as well. I was a big believer in if I looked good I'd play good, something else I got from Deion Sanders. I wore a bright-red belt, wristbands, and "spatted" my cleats—i.e., wrapped them in colorful adhesive tape, theoretically for ankle support but really for style. St. Paul's athletes weren't supposed to show off like that, so my coaches saw it as cocky and a bit rebellious. To me, it was just confidence and flair.

It was also an ongoing interest in creating my own sports fashion that started back when I'd worn multi-layered socks for protection but also as my own unique style. I'd never have guessed this would eventually lead me to producing my own sports brand. Or that I'd start designing that brand in prison!

But no one cared about my attitude or whether I was breaking tradition once football season started. I had two interceptions in each of my first three games. By season's end, I'd tied nationally for the most interceptions and was leading the country in punt returns. We made it all the way to CIF finals, where I found myself on the cover of the Whittier Daily News sports section returning a punt for another touch-down.

We ended up losing the championship by a single field goal, but we were still proud of how hard we'd worked and how far we'd come. Maybe a little too much pride. Too much arrogance. When you get used to winning like that, you start to act as if you have some kind of entitlement, and I knew I was guilty of that. The truth was, the other team just played a better game that particular night.

I started basketball season on cloud nine. Letters were coming in from big-time Division I college programs like Notre Dame, USC, Nebraska, Arizona State, Tennessee, and a bunch more, all interested in me playing football for them in a couple years. We hadn't quite won a CIF championship in football, but this had been my best year yet as an athlete, and by the playoffs we were on track to another championship win in basketball.

Then my world crashed down again. And once again, I couldn't blame anyone but myself. I had to keep up a minimum of a 2.5 grade point average to remain eligible for sports. I hadn't repeated my freshman success of being on the honor roll. With long hours of training before and after school, Friday night games, and Saturday practice, I can admit I was often sleeping in class and sketchy on my homework. But I'd thought I was doing okay until I received my spring report card. I was stunned to discover I was flunking chemistry and geometry with an overall GPA of just 1.7.

Which meant I was no longer eligible to play. I was so furious with myself I punched a wall hard enough I almost broke my hand. Not that it mattered since I ended up sitting on the bench for the entire playoffs. This was even worse because top college recruiters who'd been watching me come up the ranks of travel ball were there expecting to see me play.

One university recruiter approached to ask, "Hey, Abe, why aren't you out there on the court?"

It was humiliating to admit I wasn't eligible because of grades. Worst of all, my team lost that game. The team that beat us went on to win the state championship. With my track record, I had no doubt we'd have won if I'd been on the court. For the second time, I'd let my team down.

This had nothing to do with being lazy or stupid. I knew I was neither. It had to do with arrogance and entitlement. I hadn't bothered to put the effort into my studies that I did into sports. It went back to my over-confident mentality that everything would be handed to me because of my talent. I worked hard where I wanted to work hard and figured the rest would take care of itself. But that's not how life works. Now my selfish actions had affected my entire basketball team.

CHAPTER NINE
SIDELINED

IN TRUTH, I WAS HARDER ON MYSELF THAN anyone around me. Mom gave me a big hug and told me things would be okay. My coaches were surprisingly understanding. As usual, Oscar insisted on praying with me, adding. "Just let this be a lesson for the future."

It certainly was—and another wakeup call. As far as I knew, no one on either side of my family tree had ever been to college. If I wanted to be the first, that was on me. Mom certainly couldn't help financially. The only way I'd get there was a sports scholarship. That meant keeping my grades up to a minimum eligibility level.

Doubling down on my studies, I managed to pull my grades up to finish the year with a 3.2 GPA. Though it had been a disappointing year, I was still confident about my future. My junior season had been short, but I'd had great performances. And I still had another full year to impress recruiters.

I trained all summer and started my senior year stronger than ever. I kept an eye on my grades, determined there'd be no more drama. In pre-season, I made All American. Our team was looking great. In fact, that team would give Coach Marion Ancich his three hundredth victory, making him at that time the winningest coach in California history, a record only broken to this day by Bob Ladouceur of De La Salle High School in Concord, CA. I was once again hearing from top league schools like Notre Dame and Nebraska.

I ran onto the field for my first football game filled with confidence. I ran back two punts for touchdowns. The roar of the crowd was music in my ears. My comeback was complete.

Then suddenly I was hit by a two-ton truck. Actually a linebacker weighing three hundred-plus pounds. He landed on my right knee, tearing my lateral meniscus disc and MCL (medial collateral ligament). The pain was excruciating, and I could feel my knee hanging loosely in its socket like a puppet with cut strings. But football is a macho sport, and Coach Marion was one of the toughest, manliest coaches out there. So I wasn't about to lay in the grass moaning about how much pain I was in, much less let a stretcher carry me off the field.

I managed to push myself to my one good leg and hobble to the sidelines. By this point I'd lost count how many times I'd made the newspaper or other media as a top high school athlete. So it was no big surprise that my injury also made the Whittier Daily News sports section with the headline: "CRUZ SIDELINED, POSSIBLY FOR REST OF SEASON."

The team doctor was in agreement. He shook his head gloomily. "Sorry, Abe. But your season's over. At least for football. This might heal enough for basketball, but not any time soon. You may even need surgery."

I was devastated. But neither was I going to accept it. Not without a fight! After all, I'd made it to this point working my tail off, refusing to give up, and fighting for every inch I'd attained. One of my coaches kindly made arrangements to take me to three different specialists. Two recommended surgery. All three told me to expect at minimum six to eight weeks of rehabilitation.

Because of recovery time, surgery would put an automatic end to any sports my senior year. Mom, Oscar, and my other coaches prayed with me about making the right decision. In the end, we decided against surgery. I started rehab. Incredibly, when I went back to the specialist just three weeks later, the tear was healed. The doctor called it a miracle.

I gave thanks to GOD for healing my knee. But nothing was really the same after that. Though I played well enough and so did the team, we were eliminated in the quarter-finals. I jumped straight into basketball, where we had a good season but didn't win the championship. My grades remained decent, but it was too late to push my overall high school GPA to a level that would interest colleges without what I could bring to the table in sports.

By this point in our senior year, classmates were making choices about where they planned to attend next year. I kept waiting to hear from the big name Division 1 colleges that had been talking to me for the past two years. I even spoke with a number of coaches who headed up major programs. Some who'd talked to me in the past about a full scholarship were now inviting me to try-out for their team if I happened to attend their college. What was going on?

> "Always, always, always have a Plan B!"
>
> —Abe Cruz

Finally, one Division I football coach laid it out bluntly. "Abe, you're an incredible athlete, and I wish you the best. But with your injury, we just can't take a chance on you. Sure, the grades were a bit of a problem. But that wouldn't have been an issue if it wasn't for the injury. Bottom line, college football is a whole lot more physical than high school, and with your knee who knows how long you'd last out there?"

I received the same brush-off from Division I basketball programs that had been courting me since I'd started travel ball. I was still getting offers from Division II and III colleges, but even those weren't offering full scholarships. It was when I got back my SAT scores that I really lost it. Even without my injury, my scores weren't high enough to qualify me for a Division I college scholarship or maybe even Division II.

By the end of my senior year, I'm not sure disappointment would best describe my emotions. Lost, maybe. Confused. Angry, definitely. I'd counted on college sports being my ticket to the big leagues. To the world. Or at least to the NFL or NBA. I was now questioning the entire last eight years of my life. All those hours and days and weeks and months of training were supposed to lead to success. My future had seemed so bright. Now after all I'd endured, so much hard work, so much sacrifice, all I saw ahead was darkness. And once again, I felt this was all my fault. Well, almost all my fault. Getting injured at least had been out of my control.

The truth was that since the day Oscar sat me down and assured me I'd be a champion if I took his offer to attend All Souls, I'd never once considered a Plan B. I saw one straight route to my successful future, and that was sports. I won't say I was encouraged to neglect academics. That wouldn't be fair. That was my choice.

At the same time, the long hours of training, practice, and games, not just during the school year but all summer, didn't leave a lot of time for serious academics. And there was definitely an attitude that top grades weren't a priority for blue-chip athletes since high school and even college were just stepping-stones to the pros, where no one could care less about our GPA.

If there's one important message I'd like to get out here to young athletes, it's to have a Plan B. And that includes taking academics seriously, high school and college, because you have no idea when an injury might put an end to your dream of pro-ball fortune, glory, and million-dollar contracts.

I ended my senior year with no Plan A or B in sight. Once classes were out, I found a minimum wage retail job at Nordstrom's. Otherwise I sat around lifting weights, brooding over lost opportunities, and waiting for my future to call.

A month into the summer, I came home to a voicemail from the coach of Nebraska University, one of my original top picks. He apologized briefly that he had no scholarships available after all. "But, hey, don't worry, Abe. Someone will pick you up."

His tone was kind, but all I got from the message was "Sorry, kid, we don't want you!"

That voicemail was my last straw. I had no idea what I might be doing next year, but living at home and sharing a bunkbed with my brother while attending the local junior college was not how I'd pictured my future. I was still weighing my options when I got a call from a St. Paul teammate. He'd accepted an offer to play football at the University of Wisconsin-Stout. He urged me to send my game highlight tape to the football coach there.

It wasn't a school I knew much about, but with no other offers on the table, why not! At least I'd have a friend there. I sent the tape. Then I waited. And waited. A month before start of classes, I still hadn't heard back from UW-Stout or any other college. It felt like everything good of the last ten years since Ken Mendoza and Oscar Cepeida came into my life had come to an end.

Then the phone rang. Mom picked it up. "Hello?"

"Hello ma'am." The voice on the phone was male. "This is Coach Strop for the University of Wisconsin Stout. We are interested in your son coming to Wisconsin to get his education and play football for us."

Mom knew how depressed I'd been these last months, and I could see the excitement on her face when she passed me the phone. As I talked to the coach, I felt a huge relief and an even bigger dose of humility. I'd started out so sure a Division I school would be fortunate to have the great Abe Cruz playing for them. Now I was grateful for any opportunity at all. Finally, I was on track again to get the first college education in my family tree and resurrect my athletic career.

CHAPTER TEN
HOOKED

BEFORE I LEFT FOR WISCONSIN, OSCAR took me out for a walk around my block—and a fatherly lecture. "Abe, I've been off on my own in college so I know what it's like. It's going to be a lot different than living under your mom's authority or attending a school with strict rules like St. Paul. There's going to be a lot of temptation. Especially with girls. College girls can get pretty wild. So you need to be careful, Abraham. You need to keep yourself under control. You need to keep your faith in GOD."

To me, Oscar was the father I'd never had, so I listened politely. But something had happened to me over the last difficult years. I still believed in GOD, but I'd pretty much stopped praying. After everything GOD had allowed to happen, the loss of all my big dreams, it seemed the only person I could trust with my future was me! I was more than capable of applying my own work ethic and the mindset of a champion to get my life back on track to the great future I'd come to believe I was entitled.

Meantime, I was still in my teens, and once away from oversight, however well-meaning, I intended to have fun. And that included girls. Though I'd dated occasionally in high school, I'd been too focused on athletics to have a serious girlfriend. But I'd gained enough self-esteem—and physical fitness—to know I was as attractive to girls as they were to me.

I was a little less confident when I arrived at UW-Stout for "hell week" football camp. The upper-class football players were monsters! Huge linemen up to 6'8" and 375 lbs. They weren't just big either. They had serious athletic skill.

But they immediately made me feel part of the team, and I had something to offer too—speed and agility. I started the year playing wide receiver as a "true freshman." That meant this wasn't just my first year on the team, but my first year of college, in contrast to other new teammates who were coming in having spent their freshman and even sophomore years training to qualify.

That season I led the team in receiving and made a few game-winning catches, including one final-seconds touchdown. We ended up winning the Wisconsin Interscholastic Athletic Conference for the first time in UW-Stout history with a 14-0 season. This had now happened to me so often clear back to the Pasadena Panthers at age eleven that I'd come to believe Abe Cruz showing up at a new school went hand-in-hand with winning a first-ever school championship.

I was awarded Receiver of the Year. I'd also been doing well academically. With my great football season, I was already daydreaming of transferring to a Division I college or even the NFL.

Then basketball season started, and I soon found out that misery repeats itself as much as success. Once accepted to play football at UW-Stout, I'd sent my basketball highlights tape to the basketball coach, who'd been excited to have me on the team. But before the season started, he was replaced by a new coach who brought along his own star point guard from the college where he'd previously coached.

The new coach immediately let me know I was "redshirted." The opposite of a "true freshman," this term meant I'd be practicing with the team but not playing, so my freshman year wouldn't count as one of my four years of eligibility for college basketball. This was a common tactic if a coach wanted to season a fledgling player a bit more or had a position already filled by an upperclassman. It also meant the player could spread academic requirements over five years, making it easier to keep grades up to eligibility standards.

But for me it meant another year of sitting on the bench. I was furious, especially since I was consistently beating the other new point guard in practice, and I'm sure my attitude showed. When spring break came along, I went home instead of staying to practice like the rest of the team. After all, I hadn't seen Mom and my siblings since summer, and what difference did practice make if I wasn't going to play? But if that seemed logical to me, I returned to an irate coach who made it clear he felt disrespected and that I could forget about playing UW-Stout basketball while he was in charge.

I made it through the rest of the school year by focusing on my studies—and making money. My partial football scholarship and financial aid didn't allow for pocket money, and as athletes we spent too many hours practicing to hold jobs. I ate in the cafeteria, but with all the extra calories I burned training, I was constantly hungry. Plus there were personal needs like shampoo, deodorant, Clearasil to keep my acne at bay, not to mention decent clothing since I could no longer hide behind a school uniform.

In high school, I'd saved money by cutting my own hair and a friend's, so I started my first business enterprise cutting hair, mostly for other football players. I expanded that to personal training. With my track record in sports, I commanded enough respect that people listened when I gave work-out advice—and were happy to pay for it. It wasn't long before I was spending every weekend cutting hair or training other students.

Let me make clear I had no greed in my thoughts here. I was two thousand miles from home with no family, no friends, and no money. Getting rich wasn't even on my mind at this point, just survival and putting food in my belly. I remembered only too well picking cockroaches out of my cereal, standing in line for food stamps at the welfare office, eating a buttered tortilla as my main meal of the day. I wasn't about to go hungry again, and if that meant some hustling, so be it.

"If you act successful, people will believe it."

—Abe Cruz

At the same time, I hadn't forgotten my dream of a bright, well-paid future as a pro athlete. My time at All Souls and St. Paul and being in the homes of more affluent friends there had given me a taste for an upscale lifestyle and the expensive trappings I'd never achieve on some blue-collar salary. Or cutting hair and training out-of-shape students. Achieving that dream through the NFL or other pro sports career was still my Plan A. But after repeated setbacks, I was no longer as confident in that plan. There had to be some Plan B out there. But what?

All this matters because of my mindset as I flew home that summer for a short visit before I had to get back to pre-season football camp. While home, some acquaintances introduced me to what was called a "multi-level marketing" (MLM) company. Let me just explain briefly how an MLM works. First, it isn't a pyramid scheme. Done right, it can be an excellent and ethical business model that bypasses the standard employer-employee paradigm and makes every participant a business associate with a stake in the company. Instead of salaries, money is made through commission, both from direct sales and the commissions of lower-level associates.

That's where the multi-level comes in. Each associate recruits more associates under them to sell whatever the company's product happens to be. Those "downline" pay a commission of their sales to the "upline" associate who recruited them, who in turn pays a commission "upline" to the person who recruited them. The higher you are "upline," the more money you make beyond your own sales because more downline associates will be paying you a commission.

Commission sales are nothing new, all the way back to door-to-door salesmen offering everything from encyclopedias to vacuum cleaners. And the MLM model is nothing new, Amway, Mary Kay, and Tupperware being well-known successful examples. This was 2001, the beginning of the internet marketing boom, and already economists were predicting the upsurge of online shopping and e-commerce. Amazon, Google, eBay, and countless other companies have proven those predictions true.

So how does any of this become a problem? The FTC (Federal Trade Commission) differentiates a pyramid scheme from a legit MLM when most and even all the effort and money comes from recruiting other "downline" representatives rather than actual product sales. Typically, the "downline" participants have to pay a fee or buy a "package" to join. That buy-in is what provides profit for those "upline." Which means the main source of revenue isn't from selling a great product but enlisting others to join your "downline."

With more and more people recruited in any given area, it doesn't take long for the market to be saturated. According to the FTC, more than 95% of such recruits never earn a profit. And since recruitment, not product sales, is the main revenue source, once an area is tapped out for recruits, revenue dries up. I eventually learned that the average such company goes bankrupt within two to three years. Which isn't a problem for those at the top since they can simply walk away with their commissions.

But I had none of these statistics then—and I'm not sure I'd have cared. After all, in any pyramid, I would simply assume Abe Cruz would be on top, and if those downline didn't work as hard as me to succeed, that was their problem, not mine!

The particular company my friends were involved with was offering a new e-commerce service they claimed would soon overtake AOL. To buy in as an e-commerce "consultant" was $420 a slot. Anything related to internet services sounded legit and cutting edge. During my few weeks home, I saw kids my age of nineteen and even younger driving around in Beamers, Bentleys, Ferraris, and Lamborghinis with rolls of cash, Armani suits, and the kind of flash gangbangers dreamed of.

"So what is this?" I asked my friends. "How do you actually make money?"

Since they were all looking to expand their "downline," they were happy to fill me in. They took me to a recruiting meeting, where the speaker told us how he was already earning $25,000 a week and how with any reasonable work ethic we could do the same. To do that, I just had to pay my own $420 fee, go through training, and start doing presentations to recruit my own "downline."

They had my attention at work ethic. If these guys could earn that kind of money with a little work, I could do better. I was as sharp as they were, so why shouldn't that be me getting rich? It certainly couldn't be as hard as going up against a linebacker twice my weight. I'd finally found my Plan B that could do for me everything I'd dreamed pro sports could.

I had just one week before flying back to football camp, and I attended a presentation five days in a row. The first thing they had me doing was reading books on leadership and self-development as well as biographies of successful business entrepreneurs. Successful entrepreneurs also came in to give us lectures on self-development and entrepreneurship. Learning about men who'd turned negatives into positives made me feel powerful and that I could be part of this glamorous upscale world. And let me make clear, regardless of what happened later, the basic leadership principles I read and heard were valid and have served me well ever since.

On day seven, I did my own first house presentation, signed up two people, and received my first payment. By the time part of my percentage went to my own "upline," my payment was only $39, but it showed me the system actually worked. Besides, I'd seen some of the checks my acquaintances had received, and they were big money.

I also learned the importance of "dress to impress, dress for success." Growing up poor, I'd already learned the hard way how people will judge you based on what you're wearing. So buying into this principle was just common sense. The first time I'd flown to Wisconsin, it was in sweatpants, backwards cap, and earrings. When I returned this time, I wore a suit and tie and carried a briefcase.

The offensive linebacker who picked me up from the airport just stared. "Cruz, I hardly recognized you! What are you doing?"

This gave me the opportunity to make my sales pitch. Within a few days, I had an entire group of curious football players eager to hear about the new, improved Abe Cruz. I was still playing football, but outside of practice I'd be going to class looking like a GQ model in slacks and button-up shirt. Pulling together a half-dozen of my closest friends on the team, I showed them the company's current promotional calendar, each month featuring a top luxury sports vehicle boasting their logo.

"See these cars? These are all owned by people upline in our organization. Over in LA, thousands of associates no older than us are making fifty, even a hundred, thousand a month off this. If it sounds too good to be true, it isn't. I saw their cars and their checks. I verified that they're legit. The Better Business Bureau lists them as a skyrocketing tech company. Wisconsin is brand-new territory, so you can get in on the ground-floor."

My friends looked at the new me, listened, and bought in. They then started recruiting their own "downline." Within a few weeks, we were all making money. Since I was "upline" for all of them, I was soon raking in $1500-$2000 a week. I felt unstoppable and on cloud nine. But like a gambler in the adrenaline rush of that first big win, the reality is that I was hooked.

Hooked on the feeling of success.

And, of course, hooked on money!

CHAPTER ELEVEN
FAST CASH, FAST CRASH!

PRETTY SOON A NUMBER OF US DECIDED to move out of the dorms to share a house together. It was a typical bachelor pad with minimal furnishings beyond inflatable mattresses. I would sit on my mattress in full suit and tie making my pitch to a bunch of athletes and other students in sweats.

By now, half the football team had signed on or were asking how to get involved. At just eighteen to twenty-two years of age, we were all hungry for success and to make tons of fast, easy money. Word spread like wildfire that Abe Cruz had brought this incredible new business opportunity from LA and was making big money. I even had a few coaches ask how they could get involved.

At this time, I was still playing football too. My schedule was heavy and very regimented. Up early to train. Classes much of the day. Football in the afternoon. Then more in-home meetings in the evening. After that, I had to call my own "upline" in LA, a nineteen-year-old who'd already landed a brand-new NSX Acura sports convertible, sticker price close to $100,000, off his earnings. I'd report my progress. So many people at meetings. So many signing up.

He in turn helped me set weekly and monthly goals. It never even occurred to me there was anything odd in a nineteen-year-old holding this kind of power and position in the company. The only other job I'd held was that minimum wage retail stint at Nordstrom's, so I had no real context to judge whether this kind of money was a realistic return for what I was doing. Especially since

I was getting paid on time and in full as promised. How could this not be legit?

It wasn't long before I hit $5000 in just one week. It's hard to describe the emotional high I was on. Winning athletic championships and getting featured in newspapers and magazines had been an incredible feeling. But having a bank account and no less than $1000 walking-around cash in my pockets was a very different, incredibly powerful feeling I absolutely loved. My self-confidence soared to a new high.

Not that the cash stayed in my pocket. For the first time in my life, I could buy anything I wanted, and I did. Italian hand-crafted shoes at a thousand a pair. Gold chains and other jewelry. Hand-tailored suits, shirts, and belts. I'd had an interest in fashion since my "multi-socks" era, and now I began designing some of my own outfits, which I had custom-tailored.

The Wisconsin territory was growing so quickly the company named me a "rising star." They also sent one of their top leaders to work with me and mentor me. By now we had over two hundred "e-consultants" just in our small campus town of Menomonie, most of them UW-Stout athletes and other students. Each needed their own "downline," so the area was soon tapped out. We started moving into nearby towns and other campuses. Each weekend, we'd rent a different hotel conference facility and hold mass training sessions.

But though I and my own immediate leaders were still making good money, cracks were beginning to appear in our pyramid. For one, few of my downline associates were bringing in new associates of their own. Our local group of two hundred would show up at the hotel trainings, but they rarely brought potential recruits. Being college students on a weekend, they routinely showed up too drunk or hungover to pay attention to our training.

At the same time, the bottom tiers were starting to complain that they weren't making any of the promised quick, easy profits. I blamed them, not the system, for their lack of success. One genuine principle I'd learned in all this was that you made your own success by working hard. I was making good money now. But I was also spending long hours and all my weekends setting up meetings, pursuing recruits, making presentations—all on top of my full football and class load. Too many of these college kids who'd signed up wanted the money without ever having to put in the effort or sacrifice their time.

My leader from LA reinforced my assessment. "You can't force success on people who don't want it!"

"But it's affecting our upline," I responded. "We have to show them what they're missing."

He just shrugged. "A real leader also has to know when it's time to move on."

He then showed me one of his latest weekly checks—for $25,000! "You'll never reach this level going to school and playing football. With your drive, you could be looking at $100,000 a month. But you need to focus. You need to go all-in."

I was stunned and even upset at his suggestion. Especially since he knew my ultimate goal was still the NFL or NBA and nothing I'd earned so far compared to what professional athletes were pulling down. On the other hand, my leader hadn't steered me wrong so far. And $100,000 a month was getting into the lower ballpark of what I could earn as a pro athlete—and without all the risk and pain.

In truth, I was becoming disillusioned with the prospect of a football career. For one, no matter how fast I was or how hard I trained, my 5'9", 170-lb. frame was taking a beating from players twice my weight. Sure, an NFL career might pay millions. But if I sustained another serious injury, I could end up with nothing. And at best, a pro athlete my size could count on only a few good years. With my new business venture, I could use my brain instead of punishing my body. Even if big returns were less immediate, they could go on forever.

Beyond that, my coaches weren't very happy with me. With over half the football team part of my "downline," discussions during practice and on the sidelines were more often about what meetings we were hosting and how much money we'd made than about football. My new mentor had also introduced the practice of driving luxury cars plastered with our company logo around campus, including on the football field. He would park his personal black-on-black NSX Acura convertible in full view of our practice sessions as advertisement for players and onlookers who hadn't yet joined up.

The coach pulled me aside for a stern warning. "Abe, you're becoming a real distraction here. You want to play on my team, you keep your business away from my field. Including that car!"

"No problem." I immediately had my leader pull his convertible from sight. But that night I began thinking seriously about my next move in life. I still believed it could be football. But would it be NFL? My coach had assured me I had a chance at going pro. If not NFL, one of the growing European leagues or even Canada, Brazil, Australia, Japan.

But anything less than a starting NFL position paid at most $100,000 to $250,000 annual salary. And to ensure even that, I had to keep putting myself out there in college football, accepting routine pain every time a behemoth tailback ran over me and gambling against the strong odds of serious injury.

Meantime, my nineteen-year-old leader was already making $100,000 a month, and all he did was travel and teach leadership. While I'd never reached anywhere near that level, I'd made $5000 in one week. That would be $20,000 a month if I could keep up the momentum. Once I'd broken down the numbers, the logical decision seemed obvious.

The drawback was that I loved playing football as much as I loved making money. I was still undecided when I went to practice the next day. We were doing hitting drills, which involved slamming your body against heavy bags mounted on big sleds. Though muscular for my height, I wasn't a big guy compared to the three-hundred-pounders slamming into the sleds around me. My contribution to last year's championship had been my speed, not my brawn.

So it upset me when the coach repeatedly yelled, "Do it again, Cruz! Hit it harder! Don't be such a weakling!"

As I slammed the bag three, four, five more times, other teammates joined in. "Don't be such a baby, Cruz! What a weakling! What's wrong with you?"

In reality there was a lot fouler language and cursing involved. Never in my nine years of football had teammates or coaches yelled at me that way, and I was both shocked and angry. In the past I'd have just bit my tongue as the price for staying on the team. But with the option of a great Plan B fresh in my mind, I didn't bother trying to control myself. Snatching off my helmet, I threw it on the ground.

> "Failure and losing are not the end but the beginning of a new mission and challenge."
> —Abe Cruz

"I'm done! I'm out of here!" I screamed furiously.

Storming off the field, I headed to the locker room. Behind me, my teammates were still yelling abuse. I couldn't understand why they were treating me like this. Were they among those who'd signed up as e-consultants but hadn't seen any profits? With half the team on my "downline," that was certainly probable. Were they jealous of my own success?

The coach followed me off the field, calling, "Where are you going, Cruz? Get back here!"

Catching up to me in the locker room, he sat me down. "Cruz, what's got into you? Just tell me what's going on."

"I don't want to do this anymore," I said between gritted teeth. "I don't have to take that kind of abuse. I've got other plans for my life. I'm done here."

"No, you're not. You're just upset. Let's get back to practice." When I wouldn't budge, the coach gave up trying to calm me down. "Look Cruz, just take the day off and get some rest. I'll see you tomorrow at practice, and we can talk."

But the next day I didn't go to practice. Almost immediately, my phone rang. It was my coach. "Where are you, Cruz?"

"I told you, I'm done here." As I repeated myself, I realized I really meant it. The last twenty-four hours had made it a lot easier for me to leave all this behind—not just football but college. I was ready to move on to a new chapter in life and start making the kind of money I deserved. Hanging up on my coach, I called my leader to tell him I was taking his advice. He took me out to a high-priced restaurant to celebrate.

Sure enough, the next few months indicated I'd made the right decision. Since I was already living off campus, shifting focus full-time to my business venture proved easy. Within the week, I was expanding to different parts of Wisconsin and even into Minnesota and Illinois. I was now routinely clearing $10,000 a month. It was an incredible painless way to make money.

Even better was all the travel and speaking. I found I enjoyed teaching people how to develop into a better person as much as I did making money. I continued reading self-development books, and they basically all boiled down to one main message. Believe in yourself and go after whatever it is you want. That was a huge difference from the message I'd learned from Mom, Ken, Oscar, and my teachers and coaches at Catholic school about putting GOD first and serving others. But it was working. I was going after what I wanted, and I was getting it!

Things didn't start unravelling until my leader headed back to LA, telling me I was now more than capable of handling my territory on my own. By now I had over a thousand "downline" associates for whom I was responsible. It was soon clear I was over my head trying to micro-manage new leaders I'd never met and their presentations and sales in places hundreds of miles away like Minnesota, northern Wisconsin, and Chicago.

Then the complaints started. We'd made clear in every presentation that not every associate could count on making a profit any more than every person on a team gets to score a touchdown. Success depended on how much hard work you put in. As I'd learned playing sports, there was no instant gratification.

Of course I didn't understand that in a pyramid structure like ours the bottom tiers were guaranteed to lose no matter how much work they put in. Pretty soon I was getting more phone calls demanding a refund or threatening legal action than to sign up. I debated calling my leader. After all, he'd left because he believed I was ready to take leadership, and I didn't want to admit I was in trouble.

Then to my relief, as though he'd sensed my turmoil, my leader called me. But before I could pour out my troubles, he said, "Abe, sit down. We need to talk."

At his somber tone, my heart immediately started racing. Whatever he had to say wasn't going to be good news. Dropping into a chair, I asked worriedly, "What's going on?"

"Look, you've made a lot of money for me. For both of us. So I just want to give you a heads-up. Save your money while you can because the company is closing down."

I listened in total disbelief and shock. How could the company be closing down? What about all the people I'd talked into putting their money on the line? All the people who were counting on me? All the personal friends and acquaintances and teammates along with thousands of strangers? What would they all think of me when they found out?

"But why?" I demanded. "What happened? What's changed? Why now?"

As my leader went on talking, it became clear this was no unforeseen catastrophe. The top levels of my "upline" had gone into this venture from the beginning with an exit strategy. I understand now why people get that horrible, cringing sensation in their stomach when someone mentions the term "pyramid scheme."

I learned later this wasn't the first such business venture for the entrepreneur who'd set up our company. And it wouldn't be the last. He ended up walking away with millions before he was indicted by the FTC (Federal Trade Commission). The indictment was settled out of court for a fraction of what he'd banked and an extremely loose injunction against participating in any future pyramid-style businesses. A few years later, I discovered the FTC had shut down six more similar companies founded by the same CEO, one of which incurred a ten million dollar fine for being ruled a pyramid scheme.

"Look, Abe, I really am sorry about this," my leader wrapped up. "I just wanted to let you know while there's still time to get your money out. Just save up what you can while you can, and I'll get back in touch."

"But what about my downline? What am I supposed to—?"

The phone went dead. I never did hear back as to exactly what had happened or what I was supposed to do next. I just sat there, stunned. It was like one of those movies where your life goes before your eyes in slow motion. I'd left school for this. I'd left football. I'd traded everything I'd worked my tail off to achieve over the last nine years on the word of a guy who'd guaranteed me success if I'd work my tail off for him instead. And I'd done just that!

Only now did it occur to me that my leader had every motive to push me into leaving my dream for his—and that motive had nothing to do with securing my future. As his "downline," I was far more profitable making money fulltime for him than playing football for UW-Stout or getting my college degree. Here's another of life's hard lessons to keep in mind. Never allow someone to have that much power in your life, especially based on their word.

So what was I supposed to do now? My only ambition since I was eight years old had been to play sports. Now I was just a washed-up former football player and college drop-out. I couldn't even follow my leader's final piece of advice to bank my earnings since I'd spent all but a few thousand. I was at rock-bottom again with no up in sight.

Or so I thought.

I had no idea how far down rock-bottom could actually be!

CHAPTER TWELVE
THE GOOD LIFE

THANK GOD FOR MOTHERS! I FLEW HOME to LA feeling a complete failure. After all my hyped successes, how would Mom feel about me moving back in on her?

But I needn't have worried. Mom welcomed me with open arms, assuring me, "*No te preocupes, m'ijo* [don't worry, son]. Everything will be fine."

Not that I was too panicked at this point. After all, I still had close to twenty thousand in savings. And with no football practice or company meetings to fill my time, I figured I might as well enjoy myself.

I did make one stab at going back to college, enrolling at East LA Community College to play on their basketball team. But it felt such a step down from all I'd accomplished that I quit within a couple months. After all, where would community ball get me? Especially if it meant going back to the grind of homework and exams. I'd been out of sports and the classroom for over a year making money hand over fist. Starting back at the bottom was not where I saw myself.

Reality was, I wanted better than this. More than that, I had absolute self-confidence I could get more. I hadn't allowed other people's opinions or rules to slow me down from accomplishing things to this point, and once again I felt it was up to me to show what I was capable of. If I'd worked my way up to big, fast cash once, I could do it again. I just had to find the right opportunity.

Meanwhile at twenty-one I had time on my hands and no coaches or other authority to tell me what I could or couldn't do. I began hanging out more and more at night clubs. Fitness was still a priority, so I didn't go overboard with alcohol. I didn't smoke either, much less ever touch drugs. But I loved the glitz, music, and meeting new people, especially pretty girls. I also found a new passion—dancing. I'd never learned to dance growing up. But being an athlete gave me rhythm and flexibility. Hip-hop. Salsa. Tango. I only had to see a dance move once to copy it.

Pretty soon everyone in the clubs knew Abe Cruz. I hadn't forgotten the lessons I'd learned from my business venture. Dress to impress. If you act successful, people will believe it. I flashed the custom-designed wardrobe, expensive shoes, and jewelry I'd acquired in Wisconsin. I often dropped a thousand dollars or more in a single evening for a VIP booth where I'd party with four or five girls and other new acquaintances. People flocked to be around me, and I enjoyed being known as an up-and-coming player.

But less than six months into my new life I realized almost $20,000 had become $5000, then $2000, then less than $500. Suddenly, I was not only unemployed but broke. My party bubble had burst.

All my life, working out has been my default every time things got crazy. When I'd first returned to LA, I joined a nearby gym. I'd also begun studying Taekwondo, a Korean martial arts that focused on a lot of high, fast jumping, spinning and kicking techniques, a natural fit with my football and basketball skills. With Hollywood just down the road, my thinking was that I might have a future as the next Van Damme or Jackie Chan.

Seeing my fitness, the gym manager had almost immediately offered me a job. It paid barely above minimum wage plus commission, not the wage scale I felt I deserved, so I'd turned him down. But with no other option at hand, I took the job. I was pretty quickly frustrated. A week's check working six to ten hours a day at the gym might add up to a few hundred dollars. I'd been earning ten times that by the time I was nineteen. There had to be a quicker way to a bigger return.

One advantage I did like about working at the gym was meeting people with power, wealth, and influence, including celebrities. Whatever the downside of my stint at multi-level marketing, I'd learned a lot of great leadership lessons. So let me share another of those. Every day, all day, as long as you're around people, you're going to be judged and checked out. And you never know who you're going to meet. That person you run into just might be the one person with power and influence to completely change your life.

So you need to be the best you at all times. You need to be kind, friendly, and respectful to everyone. You should do that anyway just as a person of faith and integrity. But you have no idea of the opportunities that might open up because of a chance encounter. Or opportunities lost because you chose to be rude, impatient, arrogant, or unhelpful to someone you figured wasn't worth your attention.

Not long into working at the gym, I met a talented actor, dancer, and model who was recruiting other dancers for music videos. He suggested I audition for their next video. "If you get the job, you'll be making $500 to $600 a day for rehearsals, then another $800 a day for the actual shoot."

That was more than I'd been making in a week at the gym. The only dancing I knew was the moves I'd picked up on a night club dance floor. But I figured at worst I'd fail the audition, so why not! My mindset has always been that you can't win if you don't try.

I showed up—and nailed the audition. Learning choreography and shooting the video turned out to be great fun. Over the next couple months, I shot a total of eight music videos, making several thousand dollars each time. This led to a few minor modeling and acting gigs.

I'd also picked up from other trainers how to improve my take at the gym. Gym members might pay $40 a session for a training package, of which we trainers were paid minimum wage. A member would let his package expire, then pay the trainer directly $20 for off-the-books sessions, a bargain for the client while more than doubling the trainer's share. If not exactly legit, pretty well all the trainers were doing it. Since the gym had upwards of a thousand members and was part of a big fitness chain, our side business didn't affect the bottom line enough for the owners to care—or notice.

One of my regular clients was a real estate broker. He liked my entrepreneurial work ethic and offered me an internship in his office. I was basically training from five to eleven a.m. and evenings when clients got off work. So I had several free hours in the middle of the day. The broker set me to work learning the real estate business, filling out client paperwork, helping them with property mortgages, calling banks to arrange loans.

> "You have no idea what opportunities might open up because of a chance encounter. So you need to be the best you at all times."
>
> —Abe Cruz

Problem was, real estate is all commission, so for several months I made no money there at all. And since I had no real estate license, any commissions would be split fifty-fifty with my boss. I finally made a $16,000 commission, of which my share was $8000—for three months' work. This was still not the kind of money I needed.

Then a drought came along when I wasn't getting any more dancing or modeling jobs. I kept telling myself, "Abe, there's got to be a way you can make $10,000 a week. You've already experienced big money. You're not a brain surgeon, so what other kind of jobs make that kind of return?"

I knew real estate had potential, but where I was at, that would take years. Then one day at the gym, I heard a couple guys talking about how much money they were making doing club promotions and all the hot chicks they got to meet that way. I knew immediately this was my big opportunity. After all, I'd proved I was a hustler. I was certainly an expert on clubbing. If I could sell e-commerce packages to total strangers, I could pack out a club with paying customers. But where and how to start?

I'd been dating a girl who'd talked me into taking salsa lessons with her at a club called The Granada not far from the gym where

I worked. I talked with the owner and convinced him to let me host a hip-hop night. I'd have to guarantee at least $5000 alcohol sales from the crowd I brought in. Everything after that and a percentage of the cover charge would be my profits.

I was game for it. I began calling in favors from celebrities I'd gotten to know since moving home as well as some local basketball stars. I made up flyers, brought in a DJ, my own go-go dancers, even a porn star. We ended up with more than a thousand in attendance, and my take was $1000 for the night. Unfortunately, when you mix that many people with alcohol, someone is bound to act a fool. Sure enough, a big fight broke out at the front door. The club owner let me know he wouldn't be repeating the experiment.

Though disappointed, I understood. But I also knew I'd found my way to make real money. Bottom line, what I was earning now at the gym was just pocket change. Every club promoter I saw was making big money—not to mention all the hot chicks hanging on their arms!

Then just a few days later, a buddy called to tell me how impressed he'd been with my event at The Granada. "I've got a place in mind—Bobby McGee's over in Orange County—that's letting me do some promo nights. Wanna partner with me?"

He didn't have to ask twice. Bobby McGee's was a nightclub right across the street from the Brea Mall in Orange County and a well-known party spot for Cal State-Fullerton students and locals. I could already see dollar signs. "Sure, let's do it!"

Our grand opening at Bobby McGee's was a huge success with over four hundred in attendance. A lot of college students showed up, including friends from high school and others from schools I'd played against, so they all knew me as a local sports hero. It was a great night. But once again, alcohol mixed with crowds were a toxic combination. Right at closing time, a brawl broke out in the parking lot between football players from two different colleges.

There must have been thirty combatants. Pretty soon a dozen cop cars screamed into the parking lot. The cops starting arresting drunken brawlers. Others were jumping into cars and racing off. Fortunately, no one was seriously injured. But this was way worse than The Granada. Once the cops left, I was sure the owner was going to tell us this was the last event we'd ever hold in his establishment. I was wrong.

"I haven't had a night this profitable in a long time!" the owner told us, counting out our share of the take. "You get things straightened out with the cops. But be ready to do this again next week."

That began one of the craziest time periods in my life. I'd always been a hustler burning the candle at both ends. Now I was stretched flat out. I'd be training clients from five to eight a.m. Then I'd eat and do my own two to three hour workout, train a few more clients, then head over to the real estate office. From later afternoon till evening, I'd train more clients except for Thursday nights when I went straight home from the real estate office to eat and change for the drive to Orange County.

The club closed at two a.m., so by the time we cleaned up, collected our money, and drove back to Alhambra, it would be three-thirty or four a.m. If I was lucky, I'd have time for a nap before heading off to the gym. Otherwise I'd be up thirty-six hours or more at a stretch.

To make things even wilder, one day while relaxing by the gym's outdoor pool after a workout, I heard a man's voice call out, "Hey kid, what's your name? You should be in my show."

The speaker walked over to me. He was an older white man in excellent physical condition. I'd seen him around the gym working out but had never been introduced.

"I'm Abe Cruz," I answered respectfully, "and what show are you talking about?"

He introduced himself as Lonnie Teper. His show was the NPC Junior Cal Bodybuilding Championships, now known as Lonnie Teper's NPC West Coast Classic.

I eventually found out Lonnie was a legend in the worlds of both journalism and bodybuilding, editor-at-large of *Iron Man*, the premier bodybuilding magazine, emcee for the Arnold Schwarzenegger "Classic," an annual bodybuilding competition, and many other such events as well as host of the Muscle Beach competition, a local bodybuilding show.

That day he simply explained about his bodybuilding show and that they had a competition coming up in two weeks. "You've got great potential, kid. You should participate."

As you can imagine, I felt extremely honored to have such a top media and fitness personality recruiting me for his show. But two weeks wasn't much time to prepare, especially since I knew nothing about real bodybuilding.

"I just work out for fitness," I explained. "I wouldn't know how to compete in a bodybuilding competition."

"You don't need to know much," he smiled. "With abs like that, you're ready."

The more he talked, the more I wanted to compete. But there was one major problem—I was already booked on a family vacation on the same weekend as the contest.

That didn't stop him from trying. "Then next year."

Lonnie's confidence in me motivated me to start training even harder, and his persistence eventually paid off. Two years later, I did participate in the competition and walked away with a third place trophy. But the bodybuilding just added to the chaos my life had become. To keep up the pace, I was basically living off energy drinks—and adrenaline. Once again, I was making big money fast. And once again I was hooked on the rush.

But I'd forgotten the tough lesson I'd learned just a year back—fast cash, fast crash. Short cuts. Wild partying. Crazy hours. Like a runaway train, it was all about to catch up to me. But then, doesn't everything in life?

CHAPTER THIRTEEN
GHOSTED

NEVER FORGET THAT LIFE CAN CHANGE ON you in an instant. But how you react to changes and the impact those changes will have on your life and future depends a lot on the choices you've made up to that point.

With all the money I was making, you'd think I'd have learned my lesson and was at least building back up the savings I'd thrown away since returning to LA. After all, I'd had plenty of experience now with how quickly abundance can turn to drought.

Instead, I was once again spending it as fast as it came in. When I got my first real estate commission, I took friends out to celebrate with a total bill of more than $1200. From dropping a thousand dollars in one night to impress the girls, I was now spending several thousand. I took trips to Las Vegas. I bought more high-end clothing, watches, shoes. Anything I felt would make me look more successful. It was all show. This was the dream life I'd hoped to achieve through pro sports. And now I'd managed it at only twenty-two years of age.

You might wonder what Mom thought of my new lifestyle. Or Oscar. As before, my mom was too busy working long hours to have any idea what I was doing with my time. She was just happy I had steady employment and was contributing to household expenses.

As to Oscar, he'd welcomed me back lovingly and kindly. But I knew he was disappointed in me. Not because I'd blown the Plan A into which he'd invested so much—I knew all he really cared about was that I have a good future—but the lifestyle I was living.

He didn't see me making good money. He saw me making wrong lifestyle choices. He felt I was turning my back on GOD. He still constantly invited me to church, and I went a couple times when I stayed overnight.

But the truth was, I had no interest in church or GOD. I occasionally prayed still for GOD's blessing. But I didn't want to think about GOD or what GOD thought of my choices. I considered myself a pretty good person. After all, I wasn't doing drugs. I hadn't killed anyone. I wasn't getting drunk or into fights. I'd made something of myself. People in my world respected what I'd accomplished and my playboy image. I was sorry to hurt Oscar or disappoint him. But he no longer had any authority to tell me how to live or what to do.

Still, those choices were about to catch up to me. I'd already had some problems with the club promotion—mostly about girls. The law said you had to be twenty-one to get into a night club. I'd snuck in a twenty-year-old girl. In my mind, she was just going to hang out with me, not drink, so what was the big deal? I was back to my mindset that if I felt a rule was stupid, then it didn't apply to me. But the owner was furious as he could get shut down if the cops found out. Once again, I was letting my own selfishness hurt someone who'd been good to me.

The money wasn't coming in as fast either. I was stunned to discover my account was back down to just a few hundred dollars. Then one night all those choices came crashing down on me. I was driving home from the club about four-thirty a.m., absolutely exhausted because I'd been up almost twenty-four hours straight. I had a five a.m. client, so I couldn't even go home before heading to the gym. I'd made it from Orange County back to Alhambra and was maybe fifteen minutes from the gym when I fell asleep behind the wheel.

My last memory was seeing a red stop light up ahead. A Mercedes in front of me had stopped for the light, and I ran into its rear fender. The shock of the impact woke me right up. I must have already been braking for the light when I fell asleep because the Mercedes didn't look too damaged. The same couldn't be said for the front end of my Acura Integra.

The other driver was a petite, older Asian woman. I scrambled out of my car, apologizing profusely. "Ma'am, are you okay? I'm so sorry!"

Thankfully, she appeared unhurt. As she inspected her rear bumper, I suddenly remembered I hadn't paid my insurance bill. When she asked for my information, I begged her not to call the police, explaining I had no insurance. "Please, ma'am, I'll pay the damages myself, I promise, whatever it takes."

I was still in shock as it sunk in that I could have been killed and so could the other driver. But it didn't even occur to me to pray or thank God no one was hurt. I was just thinking of my wrecked car and where I was going to find money to pay out of pocket for both cars. My distress must have gotten through to the other driver because she took a look at the small dent in her fender and then at my face.

"It's okay, son," she said kindly. "Don't worry about it. Just be careful next time."

She got back into the Mercedes and drove off. My Acura looked pretty beat-up, but I still had clients to train. I managed to get it started and limp as far as the gym. By then I was already late for my first client, so I rushed inside. I was just grateful to have skated on the accident since I knew it was one hundred percent my fault. Halfway through the session, it suddenly hit me that getting *my* car fixed would cost a fortune. A fortune I didn't have because I'd blown it all clubbing.

From there, things just kept going downhill. After the accident, I gave up on club promotions, so that money wasn't coming in. Nor were any real estate commissions, so I was back to the "pocket change" of my gym earnings. I couldn't afford to fix the Acura, which left me without a vehicle. I caught rides with friends to the gym, real estate office, even clubs. After my high-roller lifestyle, that was a real blow to my self-image. I didn't want my new social circle to know I was broke, so I stopped dating.

Then Mom had some financial setbacks. Considering I was living with her rent-free, helping her should have been a no-brainer—if I hadn't blown all my money. From having my dream life, I'd gone to constantly stressed out about money. And once again, there was no one to blame for my situation but myself.

> "When you get knocked down, get back up, refocus, regroup, and get back to work!"
>
> —Abe Cruz

Then I fell in love. A bikini model for Hawaiian Tropic suntan lotion, she was absolutely gorgeous, and I believed she was the one. We began dating, mainly weekend evenings when I had no training clients. The problem was that I still had no vehicle and little money. Sometimes we'd double-date with my brother and his girlfriend, which solved the vehicle issue. Other times I'd talk David or my mom into letting me use their car to take her out.

Even though I was broke, I'd borrow money to throw around at the clubs. One time I tried to impress the girl by buying her a Louis Vuitton purse. It just shows where my mind was that I couldn't afford to fix my car or help Mom with her bills, but I could spend $1500 on a purse for the brief satisfaction of making a big gesture to impress a girl!

By now I'd learned that my new girlfriend was from a wealthy family and accustomed to a lavish lifestyle. I'd never brought her home to meet my mom since I didn't want her to know we lived in a small apartment. Instead, we'd hang out at her family's gorgeous home or drive places in her luxury sports car.

But eventually I had to admit I was borrowing our ride. I explained about the car accident and Mom's financial situation, then told her we'd have to take a break from dating as I couldn't even afford to take her to a movie or cheap restaurant. Her response was so understanding and sweet. Like the Mercedes owner, she told me not to worry. She had her own car, plenty of money, and didn't mind paying for our dates.

Her sympathetic reaction made me fall even more in love. And I thought she was just as into me. Then one evening as I was getting ready for her to pick me up, I received a call from her phone number. When I answered, it was one of her friends.

"She isn't coming to get you," the friend told me bluntly. "She's breaking up with you, and you're not to contact her again."

"What?" I couldn't believe what I was hearing. "Who is this? What are you saying?"

"Didn't you hear me? She doesn't want to be with you anymore!"

With that, the friend hung up. At first I felt blind-sided, stabbed in the heart. Then I decided this must be some kind of sick joke. The girl I loved would never do this. I waited a few minutes and called back.

Once again, the friend answered. "Abe, she doesn't want to talk to you. She says to tell you she's done with you."

"But why?" I asked, totally confused. "What happened? What's changed?"

"It's better this way," was all the friend said. "Don't call ever again."

For the second time she hung up. This time my heart didn't feel stabbed but as though it had exploded into a million painful shards. I was so overcome with grief and confusion I found myself flat on the ground in tears. My lack of money and broken-down car had to be why the girl was breaking up with me. I wanted to believe it was her friend who'd pushed her into this decision. But in truth I'd always known she was from a wealthy background and had expensive tastes. She'd said she was okay with my financial situation, but once she'd seen the reality of my family background and income, she'd decided I wasn't in her social class.

I never saw the girl again or even spoke to her. She "ghosted" me as they say. When I tried to call her number, it was blocked. Now I recognize I was more infatuated with this girl than truly in love (I learned the difference once I met the love of my life, my beautiful wife!). At the time I was devastated.

Worse, all the self-confidence I'd built up over the past few years evaporated. In my mind at least, I was back to that scrawny, acned misfit no girl could ever want to spend a life with or fall in love.

CHAPTER FOURTEEN
DESPERATION AND DECISIONS

FOR SEVERAL DAYS, I STAYED HOME, crying and depressed. Mom came in and hugged me. "Don't cry, *m'ijo*, you'll be okay. You'll get through this. You'll find someone better. That girl wasn't good enough for you anyway."

I guess that's what a mom's supposed to tell you, right? Hugging me again, she added, "*Dios tiene un plan para tí* [GOD has a plan for you]."

Mom said that often. When I was a kid, I'd believed her. Now I wasn't so sure. But I did know I couldn't just lie around sulking and crying. Nor was I going to let one woman's betrayal ruin my life. I had to bounce back and come up with some financial solutions quick. It wasn't that I wanted to earn enough money to win back my girlfriend. I was done with her! I just wanted to earn enough to throw my success in her face.

And to help Mom, of course.

I got on with life two ways. First, I wasn't going to let my broken heart show. I went back to the clubs—and the girls. Lots of them. I danced, flirted, and showed anyone who might care that plenty of women still found Abe Cruz attractive. But this didn't solve my financial situation. I'd grown used to a certain feeling of success, and I was determined to do whatever necessary to get that back.

So how do you make a big chunk of money fast without NFL skills or major tech smarts? I'd pretty well run through my options. While I worked at the gym for chump change—at least to my perspective—I researched for that next big opportunity. But nothing came up.

Then one Friday evening, I joined a group of friends at a club in Hollywood. That night the club was featuring a hard-body contest with a grand prize of $500. I decided to give it a try. It looked easy enough—take off my shirt, shake my hips, and flex my abs. Fifteen minutes in front of a screaming, dancing crowd, and I'd won first place. It was the easiest money I'd earned yet. As I collected the $500, I was already thinking, *Okay, where's the next contest?*

I learned of another contest the very next evening. That prize was only $100, but it took me ten minutes to win. I won several more contests, netting $800 in one week for thirty minutes of strutting a stage. I figured I'd found my new vocation.

But there were only so many hard-body contests around. The easy pickings were quickly gone. I entered one in Pasadena, but this time I found myself facing off in the final round with a guy who was clearly a pro. He gave the audience a show worthy of a Las Vegas strip joint. We'd both taken off our shirts. I was doing my normal dance routine when my opponent started taking off his pants. A mob of drunken women stormed the stage, grabbing at his pants to help get them off.

Then they were grabbing at me and screaming for me to take mine off too. I backed away, feeling disgusted and degraded. This wasn't fun anymore! And, of course, the other guy won. I walked away with a measly $50 for second place. For that kind of money, I'd already decided it just wasn't worth my pride and dignity.

Then an expensively-dressed woman approached me, a bulked-up bodyguard at her heels. She eyed me up and down. "You looked good up there, Abe, is it? You know, with that body you could be making two-three thousand a weekend in Vegas just doing what you did up there on stage. No competitions. Just straight-up earnings."

She had my interest until she explained she was a recruiter for a string of Las Vegas strip clubs. To me, taking off my shirt for a prize had been no different than being on Lonnie Teper's bodybuilding show. But a stripper act like my opponent had just rolled out? Women mobbing me like I'd just experienced on a daily basis? No way!

On the other hand, I liked the price tag the recruiter was offering, and I had nothing comparable on the horizon. I finally took her card. She told me they'd be running auditions in two weeks and gave me the address. I told her I'd be there. But over the next days, I kept having flashbacks to those drunken women rushing the stage and pawing at my pants. Surely there must be some other way to earn a good living!

> "The good thing about life is that there is no scoreboard. We might lose today, but tomorrow we have another opportunity to play again."
> —Abe Cruz

There was. That very week, I was chatting casually over my dilemma with a recent acquaintance I'd made while still flush with funds. He clearly had no money problems by the high-end sports car he drove, expensive clothes and jewelry he wore, and the cash I'd seen him throw around. When I told him about the Las Vegas offer and my reluctance to get into the stripper business, he just laughed. "Are you crazy? If you need money, you sure don't need to become a stripper. I know a way you could make in two-three days what you've been pulling down in months!"

That was even better than the recruiter had offered. I was interested but also skeptic. "What are you talking about? What kind of job offers that?"

"Look, I've got an associate who needs a driver," he explained. "Nothing full time. Just driving a car once in a while cross-country and back again. And they'll pay ten thousand round-trip. More once you show you're reliable."

I wasn't stupid. No one paid a driver that kind of money for anything legit. But I acted innocent. "What the heck would I be driving? Royalty?"

He just looked at me without elaborating. I suddenly felt like I was matching wits with Don Corleone in *The Godfather*. Then he shrugged. "Up to you. The job's there if you want it."

A strip club no longer sounded so bad. At least it was legal. I didn't want to displease my acquaintance by rejecting the offer out of hand. So I just said, "It sounds great. But I haven't made up my mind yet on Vegas. Let me think about it, and I'll get back to you."

That night I called the strip club recruiter. She was delighted to hear from me. "I've got work for you this weekend if you come up for the auditions. Two nights, fifteen hundred each."

I drove to Las Vegas in a sweet little Mazda convertible sports car I'd borrowed for the trip. When I reached the entertainment district, I could see billboards advertising lap dancers and male strippers. My stomach started to hurt at the thought of my image on one of those billboards. What if Mom saw it? Or some acquaintance reported seeing her son on display?

I'd been in plenty of night clubs, but never a strip club. The difference was apparent as soon as I walked inside. Though it would be hours before the place opened for business, guys and girls both were strutting their moves on stage wearing nothing but G-strings.

I walked through to where the recruiter was organizing auditions. She noted my arrival. "You'll be on in fifteen minutes."

I went back out to where I could see the stage. Now my stomach was really hurting, and my heart began to race. I hadn't been paying much attention these last few years to the values and teachings I'd learned from Mom and attending a Catholic school. Certainly, I hadn't been living a church-going life myself. But climbing onto that stage seemed just one step too far over the line.

Once again I had a flashback of those drunken, crazy women pulling at my pants, all sweaty, hair disheveled, lipstick and mascara smeared all over their faces. I was Abe Cruz, star athlete, business entrepreneur, player, not a piece of meat to be manhandled without my permission!

"Cruz, you're up next!"

Suddenly I just knew I couldn't get on that stage. I left the club almost at a run. Jumping into the Mazda, I floored the accelerator. I felt like I'd narrowly escaped some horrible fate. But by the time I was out of town, I no longer felt so good about my decision. My bank account was on overdraft, and I desperately needed the three thousand I'd been offered for that weekend. Now I was back where I started. Worse, in fact, since I'd wasted the gas to drive to Las Vegas and back. What now?

I was too depressed to even turn on the radio as I drove back to LA. In my mind, I kept hearing my acquaintance's voice. *I know a way . . . the job's there if you want it . . . I know a way.*

I was almost home when I finally grabbed my cell-phone and hit a redial. A moment later, my acquaintance answered.

"Hey, this is Abe Cruz. I've been thinking about your job offer. Can we talk?"

CHAPTER FIFTEEN
SOARING HIGH

THE VERY NEXT DAY, I MET UP WITH my acquaintance. First, he congratulated me for making a smart decision. "You'll be driving to the east coast and back. Making no less than $10,000 a drive. In time, a good bit more."

It was a throwback to my "upline" leader promising me $10,000 a week if I'd just do what he told me. But this time I was under no illusion that what my new employer proposed was legal. I tried to keep my voice casual as I asked, "Hey, it's not a dead body, is it?"

With a big grin, he acted like I'd been joking. "You've been watching too many movies! Nothing like that. All you'll be doing is delivering a few packages."

I knew I was pushing it, but I couldn't help asking, "What kind of packages?"

He just looked at me with that appraising stare like he'd done the first time he offered me work. Then he said, "You've done coke, right?"

"You mean, cocaine?" I exclaimed. How could he think that, knowing how I felt about fitness? "I've never done any kind of drugs!"

He nodded. "Good. That's why you're perfect for this job. Clean-cut college kid. Light-skinned enough to blend in anywhere. All you've got to do is drive a car to a location. Wait there a couple days. Then drive it back. That's it. You want the job or not?"

He'd never answered my question about what kind of packages. He didn't need to. I'd seen the movies. I knew the code.

If he didn't say flat-out, I could pretend I didn't know. To myself as much as anyone.

I nodded. I was scared. Except for those shoplifting episodes a decade ago, I'd never broken the law before, and I knew this was stepping over a big line. But I was also desperate. I tried to tell myself this was just about getting my car fixed. About helping Mom pay her bills. About building up enough cash reserve I didn't have to stress over my own bills anymore. I could step across the line just long enough to accomplish that, then walk away. It wasn't such a big deal, right?

"Yes, I want the job. I *need* the job!"

"Good. I'll contact you when I need you." He was no longer pretending to represent some other employer. "Be prepared to be gone at least three-four days."

For the next week, I worked at the gym and real estate office while waiting anxiously for a call-back. Finally, I got the call. "Okay, Abe, you're up. Meet me five p.m. at—"

He named a popular burger joint. When I arrived, he was there with a drop-dead gorgeous Latina girl who couldn't have been much older than me. She immediately took the lead. "So, Abe, what made you change your mind about driving for us?"

I figured they wanted to make sure I was no plant for the cops, so I went into big detail about how broke I was. About my mom's financial problems and how I wanted to help her like any good son. About the girl who'd ripped my heart out and how much I wanted to show her I was no deadbeat loser. About how desperately I needed money *now*.

I guess I sold my story because the girl nodded approvingly. In slightly accented Spanglish, she told me, "*Yo te puedo ayudar con estas cosas* [I can help you with all these things]. I will improve your life. I can give you a future you've never dreamed of."

Funny, that was almost what Oscar had told me all those years ago. But he'd sure had a different future in mind! Sadly, by this time I didn't care. I listened eagerly as she went on, " But first I need you to get certain things done for me. *Esto no es un juego* [this is not a game]. We're talking real business. *Mucho dinero* [much money]. *¿Comprende* [understand]?"

When I nodded, the acquaintance who'd offered me the job broke in to explain, "You leave tomorrow. Meet me back here six a.m. You'll be given further instructions then. Any questions?"

When I shook my head, the other two stood up. I watched them walk away in awe at how easy it had all been. I was no longer anxious or nervous but eager to get going. Maybe it helped to have a gorgeous female telling me she was on my side. Like I was James Bond. Or more like Al Capone. That night I went to bed and slept soundly with no nerves at all. I even dreamed of the thrill of that cross-country drive.

> "Exercise the self-motivation to get out there and do your part in coming up with a solution."
>
> —Abe Cruz

You might wonder how I could bring myself to deliver what I knew had to be cocaine when I was so hypersensitive about stripping. For one, I really didn't know much about drugs except what I'd seen and heard in the movies and music lyrics, where it all seemed to be cool and no big deal, even if technically illegal. But the truth was that my choice had nothing to do with morality. It was about my self-image. To put myself out there as a stripper, maybe even end up on a billboard in a G-string for all the people I'd once impressed to see—no matter how well it paid, it just wasn't me.

Contrast that to my new employer, who'd always projected an image of a wealthy, successful business entrepreneur. *That* was the image I'd yearned for since attending my first business seminar. And if a short stint discreetly delivering packages I could pretend to know nothing about could get me there—well, it wasn't like I'd be committing murder or theft or even hurting anyone. I knew Oscar would be deeply disappointed in me, and I had no real illusions GOD would approve. But I'd long since quit worrying about Oscar's approval or thinking about GOD. Bottom line, I knew what I'd just chosen to do was wrong, but I didn't really care anymore.

When I showed up the next day in the burger joint parking lot, my new employer was already waiting in his car. To my disappointment, his gorgeous female companion wasn't with him. Waving for me to get inside, he handed me a car key and indicated a 350Z silver Nissan sports car parked just a few slots away.

"There's your ride. Take the I-10 to I-15 towards Vegas. Don't speed. There's no rush. Last thing we want is you getting stopped by any cops. A couple hours out, I'll call you and give you further directions."

He then gave me a burner phone. "Use only this. Leave your own phone home or pull the battery. No outgoing calls except as instructed. And here's for gas, food, and a hotel."

He handed me six hundred dollars cash, then added a business card with the name and number of a Beverly Hills attorney. "If you do get pulled over, keep it cool. Remember you're just a college kid, no priors, minding your own business. But if you have any trouble, keep your mouth shut and call this number as soon as you get a chance. That's it. Don't tell the cops anything."

Walking me over to the 350Z, he laid a hand on my shoulder. "Hey, relax, Abe. It's all good. You're on a nice, little joy ride, and when you get back, I'll have ten thousand waiting for you."

It's hard to describe how I felt as he walked off and I climbed into the Nissan. Scared, sure. Nervous, yes. But also happy. Excited. Confident. Like that gorgeous Latina had promised, the solution to all my problems was waiting for me at the end of this ride. A great new future.

Since the east coast was at least a thirty-hour drive, I'd brought a stash of energy drinks as well as some CDs of my favorite rap artists. The lyrics were always going on about the drug life, so I figured I might as well educate myself on this new game I'd suddenly found myself involved in. That I could even *think* of what I was doing as a game shows how immature and stupid I really was instead of the sophisticated player I considered myself to be at twenty-three years old.

But I'd barely got myself settled into the soft, comfortable leather of the driver's seat when I saw I had a problem. The 350Z Nissan sports model was a stick shift, and I'd never driven a manual transmission.

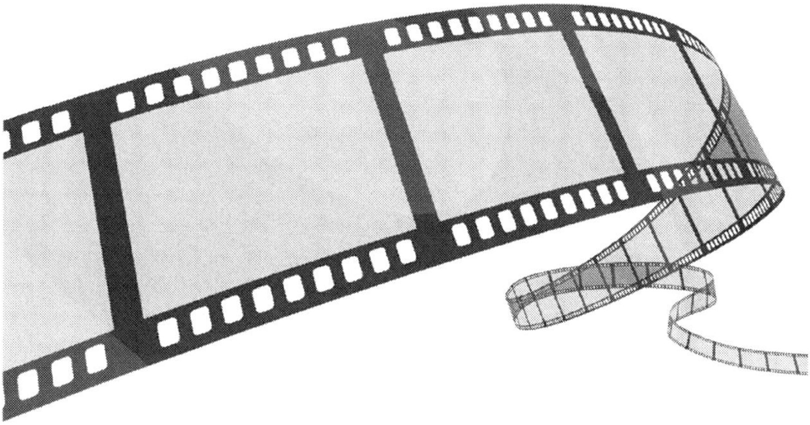

Early photo with my mom.

David and I with Big Brother Ken Mendoza and his wife Rose.

Pasadena Panthers Jr. PeeWee Football. I'm on the top row between the coaches.

In my Panthers football outfit.

With Oscar Cepeida family: top row left-to-right are my cousin Olivia, Oscar and wife Ofelia, David, myself, and cousin Orlando. Front row are cousins Amanda, Oliver, and Omar.

In action on the court (#22) playing basketball for St. Paul.

SPORTS

Thursday, March 13, 1997

St. Paul at a Crossroads
Swordsmen get a close-up look at Baron Davis

By Robert Morales
STAFF WRITER

Baron Davis is the player most asked about when discussing the Crossroads School boys basketball team.

Davis, a heavily recruited 6-foot-2 senior guard, averaged 24.2 points and 7.7 rebounds during the regular season.

"He is a very good player. Actually, they are a very good team," St. Paul coach Randy Castillo said.

Davis and the Roadrunners will play host to St. Paul at 7:30 tonight in a CIF Southern Regional Division IV basketball semifinal at Loyola Marymount University.

Crossroads (28-3) is the division's top seed.

Tonight's winner will play for the Southern Regional championship Saturday at Cal State Fullerton. The winner there will play the Northern Regional champion for the state title March 22 at Anaheim Arena.

Castillo and his players are eagerly awaiting the opportunity to play against one of Southern California's top collegiate recruits. Davis is being recruited by UCLA, among other highly-respected NCAA Division I schools.

"They have seen Davis play and they have heard of him," Castillo said of his players. "They are just excited to be playing Crossroads and to play against this kid. And, they get an opportunity to play one more game.

"But we do have a tough task ahead of us."

Davis helped Crossroads to a victory over Santa Ana Calvary Chapel in the Southern Section Division IVAA title game last Friday at UC Irvine. The Roadrunners defeated Coronado, 81-41, Tuesday in a first-round state tournament game.

The Swordsmen (15-13) defeated Twentynine Palms to win the Southern Section Division IVA title last Friday. They defeated Corcoran of the Central Section 42-41, Tuesday in a first-round state tournament game.

Abraham Cruz, St. Paul's freshman point guard, will defend Davis at least some of the time, Castillo said. Cruz has come up with numerous steals during

Cruz and his teammates watched Davis play Friday because Crossroads' game against Calvary Chapel preceded St. Paul's with Twentynine Palms.

"I saw him before our game," Cruz said. "He's going to get what he's going to get. So we're going to try and stop his teammates. We want to make him do it all.

"If we stop his teammates, we have a good chance at winning the game."

Castillo said he considered playing a 2-3 zone defense, since Calvary Chapel used it and had some success. But he said during Wednesday's practice that he probably won't do that.

"With only a day to prepare, we might have to go with what got us here," Castillo said. "And that's our man-to-man defense."

Davis isn't by himself on this Crossroads team, which has won back-to-back Southern Section titles. Cash Warren (6-1, 16.9 points per game average), the son of former UCLA star Mike Warren, will start at the other guard spot.

Photo by M. LEAFDALE HIDE
ST. PAUL'S Abraham Cruz and the Swordsmen play Crossroads tonight.

Featured playing basketball for St. Paul in local newspaper.

With my mom, sister Marta, and brother David.

In my #22 St. Paul high school football uniform.

Making an interception (#22) playing for St. Paul football team.

High school graduation day with my mom and younger brother David.

My new upscale look as network marketing associate.

Prison mug shots.

> Being Prepared is The Key to Success!
>
> - START FOREVER FAITH - Brand to Mac : Inspire the World
> - Prison system workouts Device
> - Film Actor producer, writer
> - TV - Actor, writer, producer
> - Cover of Magazines Worldwide
> - Speaking to the Youth / Motivational speaker
> - Diddy Stick
> - Dark Justice - Comic Book / Movie
> - Philanthropy - Giving back / because God blessed me

"Business Plans from Prison" written on anything I had.

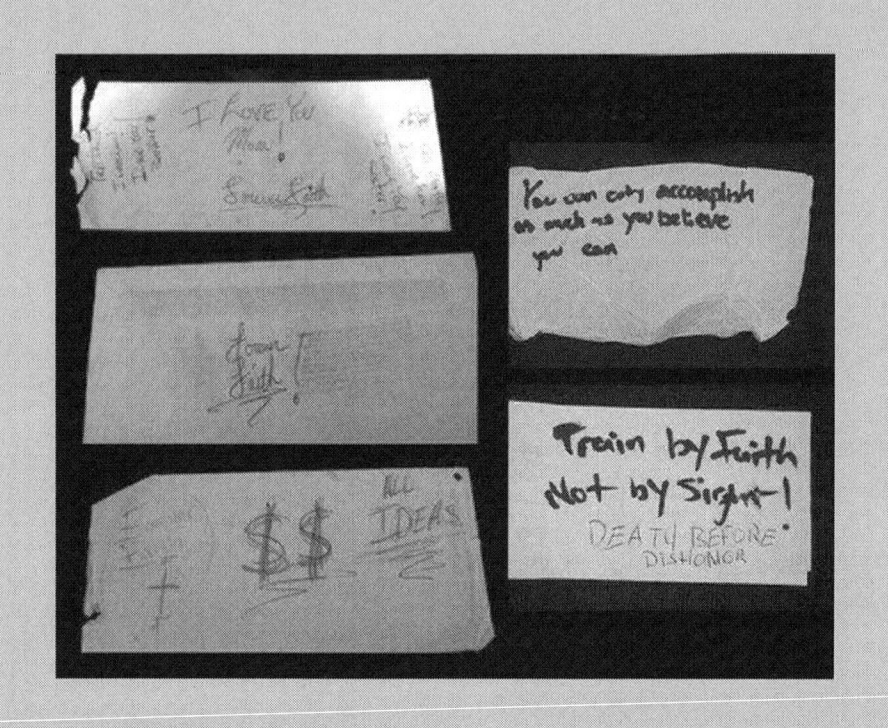

Each vision God gave me.

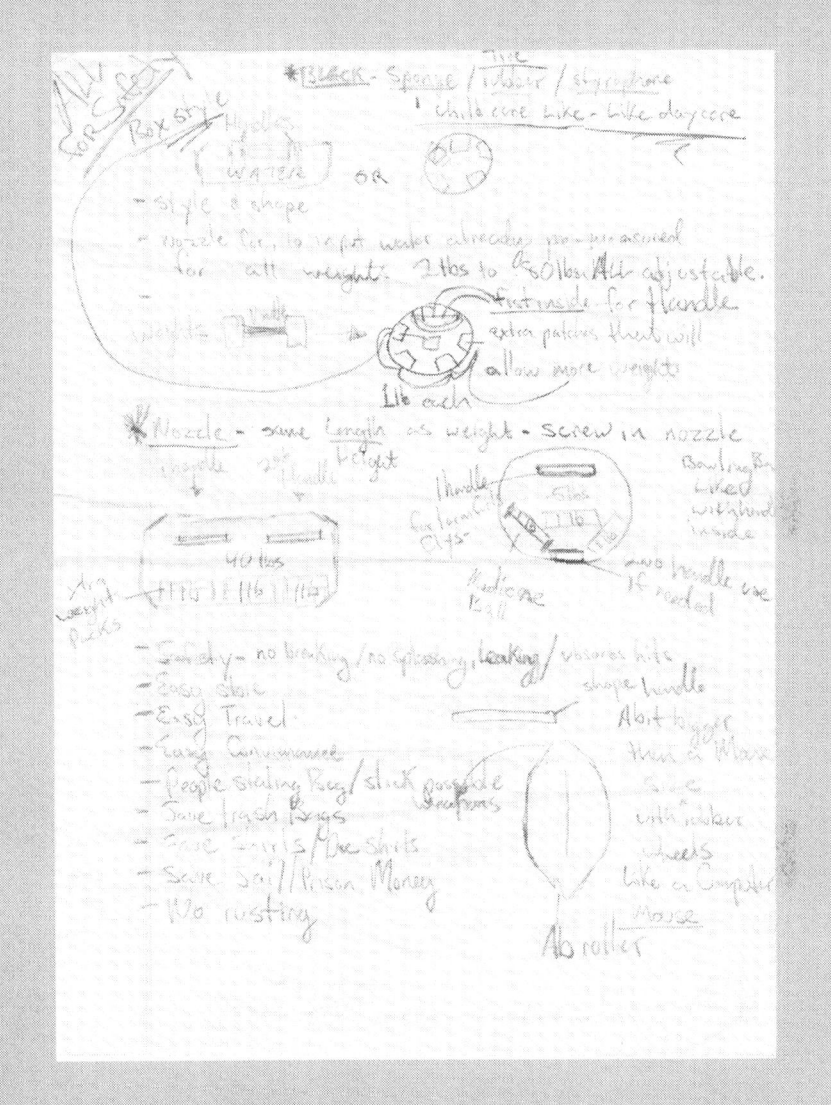

"Business Plans from Prison"
written on anything I had.

Dark Justice comic book created in prison.

Prison workout using plunger sticks and trash bags filled with water. Years later my method was featured in this *Fitness* Magazine.

Front-page interview in the Tulsa World newspaper.

Wearing my ankle monitor while working as a trainer at the gym.

From Prison to Forever Faith interview in *Fit & Firm* magazine.

With my Pops, Fred Bassett, on the red carpet introducing *Forever Faith*.

My Pops, Fred & his wife Janet.

FOREVER FAITH
TINY LISTER & ABE CRUZ
Film Comedy Sketches with
Director JOEL DE FRANCE
April 2015

A comedy film sketch with Tiny Lister, one of several forays into acting.

More covers and features from both fitness and mainstream magazines.

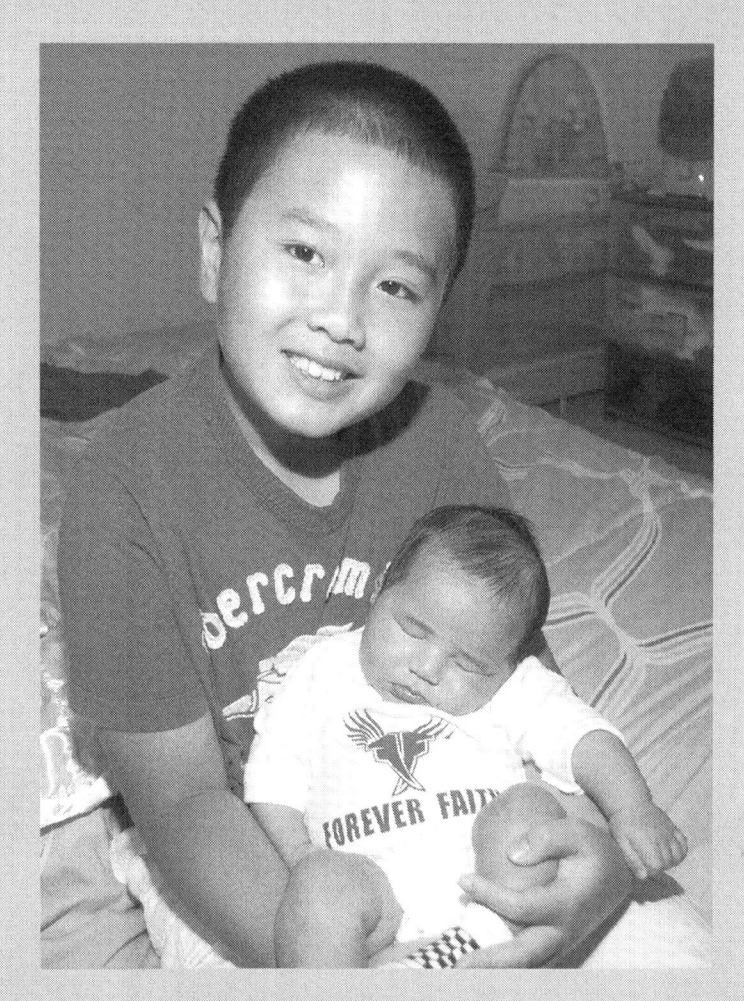

My son Joshua with big brother Justin one day old wearing his Forever Faith onesie.

First full family photo with my beautiful wife Ha, big brother Justin, and Joshua eight months old.

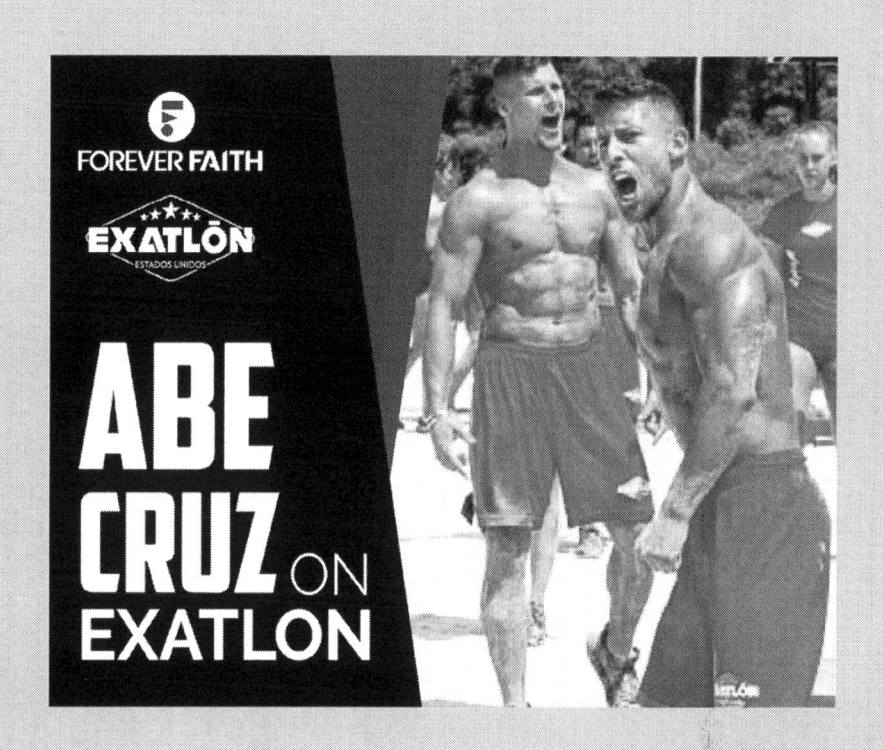

Participating in EXATLON, Telemundo's top-rated show, as T3 on Team Famosos.

With my Forever Faith mentors and team—Marc Harper, me, Fred "Pops" Bassett, and Jim Spargur.

With some of the great models for our Forever Faith clothing line 2020.

FOREVER FAITH

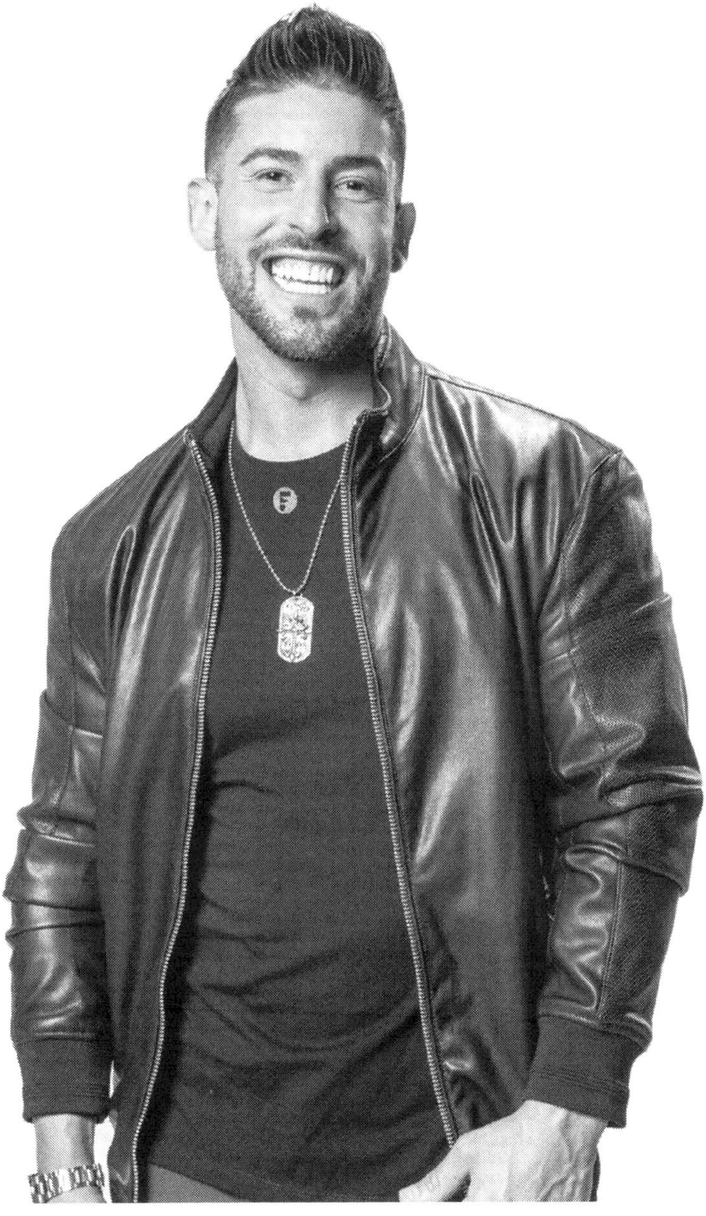

CHAPTER SIXTEEN
REALLY HOOKED!

CALLING MY NEW EMPLOYER ON MY NEW burner phone and telling him I'd have to bail because I couldn't drive the car he'd assigned me was not an option I considered. Here's where the old Abe Cruz self-confidence kicked in. If at eleven I could figure out complex football moves from watching pro sports, how hard could a stick shift be?

Working the gears and pedals, I stopped and started my way around the parking lot, almost empty at this early hour. I might have stripped the gears a few times, but within a few minutes I had it figured out and was ready to hit the road. Sure enough, by the time I reached the interstate, I was cruising.

Two hours later, my boss called. "Okay, you're heading to Oklahoma City. Take this exit and get on I-40."

For the next thirty-odd hours, I kept the Nissan on cruise control, listened to rap music, and drove. I stopped only for restroom breaks, more energy drinks, food, and to fill up the gas tank. Every few hours, my boss would call to give me new directions which way I should go. Only when I crossed the Ohio border did he let me know my final destination would be Columbus. I was to take the mall exit and park at a particular spot in the parking garage outside Nordstrom's.

"You'll see a red car parked off to your left." He gave me the license plate number. "Key's under the driver's seat. Take that car, find a hotel, and do whatever you want to do for the next couple days. You'll get a call when things are ready for the return trip."

I followed his instructions, and everything was exactly as I'd been told. Checking into a hotel, I spent the next two days working out in their gym, swimming in the pool, trying out fancy restaurants, and loafing. On the third day I received a call that the Nissan was ready for the return trip.

"Be safe and take your time," my boss reminded me. "You're carrying a lot of cash. You don't want any attention."

Which pretty well confirmed I'd driven east loaded with cocaine and was now taking payment in kind back to LA. Driving to Nordstrom's, I parked the red loaner and climbed back into the Nissan. I could see no indication anything had been removed or put back in. That was fine with me. I didn't need or want to know anything except the payment I was expecting.

> "Smile, speak respectfully, show humility—it works every time."   —Abe Cruz

The trip back was as uneventful as the trip out. I drove straight through, feeling totally relaxed, singing along to my favorite rap CDs. Now that I was in the game, the lyrics took on a whole new meaning. Blow was cocaine. A key was a kilo brick of dope. Mule. Making a drop. Stash house. Those all described what I'd just done! Cassidy's "I'm a Hustla'" might as well have been a primer in getting rich transporting and street-marketing narcotics right under the eyes of the cops. The language was raw, violent, and explicit, but instead of being repelled, I found it thrilling to find myself part of this exciting, lucrative global underworld. By the time I was back in LA, I felt I'd gotten an education in my new business.

I followed instructions to leave the Nissan where I'd picked it up in the burger joint parking lot. When no one was there to pay me, I was worried I'd been stiffed. But the next day my acquaintance tracked me down and handed me a brown paper sack containing $10,000 in cash. "Good job, Abe. You earned this. I'll be in touch."

And just like that, I was $10,000 richer. I felt more paranoid carrying that cash home in my backpack than driving the 350Z almost five thousand miles. I was still in disbelief over what I'd done these last few days and how easy it had all been—like a movie script instead of a real illegal enterprise. I gave Mom a thousand bucks to help with the rent and bills. I could hardly tell her I'd earned it driving cross-country with drugs, so I made up some story about going off somewhere on a modeling gig.

With the remainder, I went car shopping. Dealers were reluctant to sell to a twenty-three-year-old with no credit history. But for a $5000 down-payment, they let me leave the lot with a brand-new 5 series BMW tricked out completely black-on-black with rear, brake, and other lights switched out from red and orange to crystal-clear white and super-dark limo tint windows. Straight gangsta! This time I took no chances, paying for full insurance coverage before driving away.

Which left me less than a thousand bucks. I was no longer nervous about running drugs but about how long I'd have to wait for another call. I returned to reality, working at the gym, going to the real estate office, running my off-book training sessions. But it felt like just putting in time. I was ecstatic when less than two weeks later the burner phone rang.

"It's go-time!" My boss spelled out his instructions—same travel protocol, same state, new final destination. "This time your take's fifteen."

Meaning $15,000! He didn't bother this time with all the phone calls, just gave me a route to follow and told me to call for my drop site when I exited at the final destination. The trip went as smoothly as the first. I spent a couple days just chilling at a hotel, working out, eating great steaks at Outback Steak House—the good life.

Heading home, I felt totally relaxed and wasn't even giving a thought to cops. About one a.m., I was flying through Indiana, listening to Lil' Wayne's *The Fireman*.

"...Your new girlfriend is old news. You ain't got enough green and she so blue. Cash Money Records, where dreams come true. Everything is easy, baby, leave it up to Weezy Baby. Put it in the pot, let it steam, let it brew. Now watch me melt; don't burn yourself, 'cause I'm the Fireman, Fire, F-Fireman..."

By now the lingo was as much a second language as Spanish. If I didn't relate to the Fireman's self-destructive "melting" and "burning" on crack, I could sure relate to not having enough "green" for a stuck-up girlfriend and doing whatever it took to get the cash to make my dreams come true.

The blasting music and anticipation of what this trip would net me had my adrenaline so pumped up I didn't even hear the police siren. Then blue-and-red lights started flashing in my rearview mirror. I began to panic as I pulled over to the shoulder of the road.

"Chill, Abe!" I told myself, taking a deep breath. "It's no big deal. You've got this."

Turning down the music, I rolled down my window. By then the highway patrol officer was walking over, hand on his gun, flashlight probing my face. "Driver's license and insurance, please."

I was already apologizing as I dug them out. "I'm so sorry, officer! I always listen to music to stay awake when I'm driving late, so I didn't hear you right away. I know I was probably speeding."

"You were going close to ninety miles an hour," the officer said sternly. "Have you been drinking?"

"Just energy drinks to keep me awake." I showed him the one I'd just emptied. "I guess it got me kind of pumped up so I wasn't watching my speed. I'm really sorry. I've just got a few more miles to reach my hotel for the night."

The officer walked back to his cruiser to run my info, then returned. "Okay, son, it's late so I'm just going to give you a warning. You slow down and drive safely."

"Thank you, officer," I said fervently. "And you have a great night!"

I couldn't believe my luck as I drove away. Smile, speak respectfully, show humility—it worked every time! But I immediately set the cruise control just under the speed limit. My nerves couldn't take another close call like that.

When I got back to LA, my boss phoned for me to deliver the Nissan at a house instead of the burger joint parking lot. Following his instructions, I drove straight into an open garage. I spotted my boss as the garage door clattered shut behind me.

"How was the trip?" he asked when I climbed out of the vehicle.

"All good. I did get pulled over, but the cop let me go." I explained what had happened, a little worried this might be the end of my new job.

But he took the news more casually than I expected. "These things happen. If you're here, that means you handled yourself well. Great job. Now sit down and relax."

I found a seat on a nearby stool. Then to my surprise, he started breaking down the 350Z right in front of me like it was some kind of Transformer vehicle. There were small secret compartments everywhere—in the trunk, the seats, the doors. He finally straightened up. "Well, it's all here. $500,000 cash."

I was speechless. I'd never seen that much money at one time in one spot in my life, and in truth I wasn't really happy to have seen it now since that meant I'd clearly earned some trust. If these guys were feeling comfortable enough to start revealing their secrets, they might ask me to do more things for them, and I had no interest in rising in the ranks of this drug game. All I'd wanted was to make some quick money and walk away.

All the same, I was up $25,000 in just a couple weeks, and I sure wasn't ready to quit yet. I had a timetable in mind. Pay off my car. Put a down-payment on a condo so I could move out of Mom's apartment. Pay off all outstanding bills—hers and mine. Find a lucrative business where I could keep up my lifestyle legitimately. Then I'd worry about how to safely walk away from all this.

Handing me a bundle of cash, my boss gave me a sharp look like he knew what I was thinking. "So when are you going to leave this behind?"

If I'd said, "right now," I really don't know if I'd have walked out of that garage alive. But that thought didn't even cross my mind. I liked the taste I'd had of this exhilarating new life, and I was definitely not ready to let go.

"Not anytime soon," I answered. "Eventually maybe when I make some big money."

"You stick with me, and that'll happen soon enough," he assured me. "You do well, and we'll maybe put you on one of the bigger runs. Those can run to sixty grand a pop."

Looking back, I'm sure my new boss knew exactly what he was doing and that this wasn't the first time he'd dangled just the right bait to get a kid on the hook, then reeled in the line to keep him there until he was in too deep to get out. He certainly had me! I wasn't just hooked but *really* hooked. Not just on money and the adrenaline rush of skating on thin ice and getting away with it. I was hooked on the whole lifestyle, and I was no longer sure I ever wanted to get free.

CHAPTER SEVENTEEN
OUT OF CONTROL

My good intentions of saving up and moving out into my own place went out the window almost immediately. The money was once again flowing through my fingers as fast as I could make it. Forget paying off the Beemer or that down-payment on a condo. Everyone needs a Rolex, right? Another upgrade on my designer wardrobe with all the top Italian brands. Then there was the jewelry and designer sunglasses. Not just one of each but a different set for every day of the week.

Though getting back at the girl who'd broken my heart took most of my earnings. I'd travel to Las Vegas and spend $5,000 to $10,000 in a weekend. Or drop several thousand for a wild night at the Playboy Mansion. Always with a new group of gorgeous woman crowding around. Somehow, popping a bottle of expensive champagne always brought them running.

Plus, I usually managed to find some reason to take my shirt off everywhere I went. I knew I looked good. And rich. And successful. Too bad my ex-girlfriend was never there to witness what she'd thrown away. I could always hope she saw me on social media or some friend would get word back to her.

Every two to three weeks, I'd get a call to make another trip. I no longer had any worries about the law catching up to me, only about too much time passing before my next payday. Within a few trips, I was earning $20,000 a run. I did occasionally get pulled over and ended up with a couple tickets for speeding, but that no longer sent my heart jumping out of my chest. I just put on my clean-cut, respectful college boy act, and they always bought it.

My one big scare was when I was pulled over outside Oklahoma City. The highway patrol officer didn't look impressed by my act. Examining my California driver's license, he demanded with a heavy southern accent, "What are you doing out here, boy?"

Since I was right down I-44 from the Oklahoma State University satellite campus, I spun a tale about visiting my girlfriend there and that I was now heading back to classes in LA. He took a closer look at my tank-top, shorts, athletic build, and deferential smile and didn't even blink before telling me to move along and have a safe trip.

By this time I'd quit any other jobs, though I kept my hand in at the real estate office. But looking good was important to me, so I still went to the gym to work out and kept up with my Taekwondo training. In fact, I'd added another new element to my fitness program—anabolic steroids.

This started because of a work-out injury. I'd been told the steroids would help my body heal faster, so I purchased them from someone selling at a night club. They worked, and I liked what they did to my muscle mass. I knew steroids could have side effects and weren't strictly legit self-prescribed. But I'd heard that plenty of pro athletes and bodybuilding stars bulked up that way, so why not me?

Pretty soon I'd put on a good twenty percent additional muscle mass and was in the best shape of my life. One side effect of the steroids was a return of my acne. But now I could afford treatments like Benzoyl peroxide and Accutane to keep the acne in check.

Looking back, I was crazy out of control during this season, though I'd never have admitted that. I still thought of myself as a good person. I mean, I wasn't violent or reckless or being a jerk to anyone. I was helping my mom with rent and bills. In my eyes, I was a hip, sophisticated playboy with money in my pocket having a good time. I just didn't believe in rules anymore. Or at least that they didn't apply to me. I even had a belt buckle custom-designed for about $500 that read "Natural Born Hustla."

You lose track of time when you're living like this. Before I knew it, eighteen months had gone by. I was still nowhere near the kind of money I needed to quit this life. In part, because of my spending. But the big payouts hadn't happened either. Now I was the one pushing my boss to put me on a bigger run—whatever that actually entailed—because I wanted the higher payout. But so far I'd been kept on the same California-Ohio route.

That said, they were definitely trusting me more. They no longer wasted time having me switch cars in a parking garage but would just have me deliver the 350Z to some gated house or upscale condo. On one trip, they let me stay in the garage while they opened the secret compartments and lifted out white kilo bricks wrapped in shrink-wrap and duct-tape. By this point, all I saw was new opportunities. That this life might hold danger didn't even cross my mind.

> "When all you see is opportunity, you miss recognizing possible danger." —Abe Cruz

It was more than a year in when that changed. I'd been driving for over twenty-four hours straight and was starving. Just a few miles from my final drop point in Columbus, I stopped at a 24-hour Waffle House to grab my usual steak-and-eggs combo. The area was pretty much a slum like the hood I'd grown up in, maybe not the best place to park a fancy sports car, especially at well after midnight. But I was too hungry to care. I finished eating, paid my bill, then headed back out to the Nissan. Just as I was unlocking the car, I heard footsteps rushing at me from behind.

Instinctively, I spun around and threw my hands up. A large man was coming at me. Light from the restaurant parking lot glinted on a big knife he'd raised to stab at me. As the knife came down, my Taekwondo training kicked in. Sidestepping, I blocked his blow with one arm while my free hand grabbed the arm with the knife.

The adrenaline rushing through me gave me enough strength to literally rip his shoulder from its socket. I heard and felt it as I threw the man back into some bushes. I felt no guilt at all. The man had been trying to kill me and jack my car. Nor did I even consider calling the cops. In a hood like this, who knew how long that would take? And I had no interest in explaining what I was doing there, even if they took my word that I was just an innocent victim.

But when I got back in the Nissan, a searing pain in my right triceps told me I hadn't escaped unscathed after all. Fortunately, it was winter so I was wearing a thick, long-sleeved sweater. As I pulled out of the lot, I could feel the wool getting heavy and wet with blood. I couldn't drive to a hotel this way, and I sure wasn't going to an emergency room, so I called my drop point to let them know what had happened.

They told me to come straight in. When I got there, several men with drawn guns stepped outside, looking around to make sure I was alone and not being followed. Once they verified I was telling the truth about my injury, I was given some first-aid supplies and left to take care of myself. It turned out I had a gash about four inches long. It wasn't deep, and I was able to stop the bleeding. They let me stay the night instead of sending me to my usual hotel. Through an open door, I could see stacks of money being bundled to replace my east-bound cargo. My hosts made clear I wasn't to go anywhere near there.

That was fine with me. For the first time I wasn't feeling good about making another successful run. My arm burned so painfully I couldn't sleep, and when I closed my eyes, I had flashbacks of that knife coming at my chest. If I'd heard the man just a few seconds later or been a little slower in reacting, I'd be dead right now!

And why had he attacked me? Was he just some homeless bum or crack-head who'd seen what looked like easy pickings? Or had he targeted me because he knew about my cargo? No, that was crazy as even I hadn't known I was going to stop at that Waffle House. But I couldn't shake that horrible feeling of adrenaline and heart-stopping terror I'd felt fighting for my life.

The next morning when I left, my host told me I should get myself a gun or combat knife before any further trips. That made me feel even worse. The club life, cross-country treks, easy money—it really had started to feel like a game. And like a game, I'd started to take my invincibility for granted. Did I want to be in a business where I had to carry a gun or knife to guarantee my safety?

Driving back to LA, I was no longer relaxed and enjoying myself but edgy and constantly looking over my shoulder. Thankfully, no cops pulled me over on that trip, as there's no way I could have passed for a carefree college kid. My arm hurt horribly, and for the first time in months I thought about just walking away from all this. But I needed at least one big score before I could quit. Otherwise, I'd just be back where I started, twenty-five now but once again broke with nothing on the horizon.

I asked my boss again about moving up to a higher paying gig. My heavy mood lightened and I forgot my worries about safety when he responded, "There's nothing available at the moment. But, sure, just give the Nissan a couple more trips, and the next opening is yours. At sixty grand just for starters."

"I'll be ready," I assured him. "Just let me know when."

But in fact, the Nissan only had one trip left. And so did I.

CHAPTER EIGHTEEN
BUSTED

THE NEXT CALL CAME LESS THAN A WEEK later. The trip east went so smoothly I'd thrown off my jitters by the time I reached my destination—especially since this time I'd been promised a full $35,000 as my take for the trip. As usual, I wasn't given my drop-off point in advance. But when I exited in Columbus, I met up with a bright-yellow sedan I'd been told to expect. I followed the sedan to an upscale two-story townhouse with a two-car garage. A number of luxury cars were parked along the curb, but I drove into the privacy of the garage.

My gory experience on my last trip must have dispelled any remaining distrust as this time my hosts put no restrictions on my movements. I walked into the money room, where precise stacks of one dollar bills through one hundred covered tables at least a couple feet deep. In the next room, white bricks were being carried in from the Nissan.

My club life had desensitized me to flocks of scantily-clad gorgeous women. Even so, half-a-dozen girls in nothing but panties and bras shrink-wrapping bundles of money and stacking up bricks of cocaine sure got my attention. At least that many guys with guns were walking around, keeping an eye on what the girls were doing. Their calm reminded me that this operation had been operating safely far longer than I'd been driving for it. It was silly to get my nerves up.

I slept well that night in one of the upstairs bedrooms, dreaming only of the $35,000 I'd been promised. By the time I was halfway back to LA, I was already making plans how to spend my biggest payday yet. Though I was still jumpy enough to make sure I stayed under the speed limit as I curved south along Oklahoma City's west side to jump on I-40 for a straight shot west to California.

Which was why those two Oklahoma Highway Patrol cruisers sliding out of the bushes right on my fender was such a shock. Even then I was confident I could talk my way out of this like I'd done every other stop—until the DEA showed up in their black SUVs with drug-sniffing dogs and their handlers. That's when I knew I was busted!

I've already told you about the arrest. But I was still hoping I wasn't in too much trouble. After all, I had a clean record since Mom had made sure that CVS where I'd shoplifted never filed charges, and I didn't actually have any drugs in the car. Just ferrying a stash of money wasn't illegal, was it?

I don't know when I began to realize this was no chance traffic stop or even some over-zealous profiling but that these guys knew exactly who I was and what I was doing there. Standing handcuffed up on the hillside next to a highway patrol trooper, I heard someone call out, "We've got something! We got a hit here!"

Even then I assumed they'd just found the hidden money. A few minutes later, the trooper escorted me down the hill and into the back of his cruiser. I saw a DEA agent climb into the driver's seat of my vehicle. The cruiser pulled away, followed by the Nissan. I expected to be driven to a police precinct. Instead, the cruiser stopped again just a few minutes later.

We were in an industrial area, unpopulated at this late hour of night—or early hour of morning. A moment later, we drove through a huge open door into the loading/unloading area of a warehouse. The Nissan pulled in behind us followed by the black SUVs filled with DEA agents, dogs, and their handlers.

Two police officers hauled me from the cruiser and led me around a corner to a pipe running up one wall. Unfastening my handcuffs, they wrapped my arms around the pipe and refastened my cuffs so that I was in effect chained to the pipe. They left me there. A few minutes later, I heard the loud buzz of a chain saw and a droning whine like some kind of drill.

I had no doubt they were sawing my car open. But I was suddenly too exhausted to care. I'd been driving for over twelve hours, and there was nothing I could do anyway. Sliding to the concrete floor, I leaned my head against the pipe and closed my eyes.

I don't know how much time passed, but it couldn't have been more than a couple hours because it was still dark out when a hard hand on my shoulder shook me awake. A DEA agent was standing over me. "We found the money and the dope, kid. You're busted! You're going to jail, so if you know what's good for you, you'd better get talking."

When they led me around the corner, I could see the 350Z in pieces with doors, seats, spare tire, and the ripped-up trunk-bed all scattered across the concrete. I could also see stacked bricks of shrink-wrapped money but nothing anyone could conceivably mistake for drugs. I was dazed and confused as an officer deposited me back into a cruiser. Okay, so they'd found the money. That I'd expected. But how could they have found drugs?

A kilo brick of cocaine was big money. There was no way those men at the stash house would have left one behind. So had these agents or even the cops planted the drugs just to get me on a higher charge of trafficking cocaine? I'd certainly seen plenty of such stories on TV and in the movies.

I never did learn the full truth. But I eventually found out that the house where I'd stayed the night had been under surveillance for some time and was raided shortly after I drove away. Did the DEA have an inside informant or undercover agent who'd made sure a kilo remained behind in one of the hidden compartments? Or had it really been carelessness? Or planted? Or were the agents just lying about finding the cocaine to get me to confess?

It probably didn't matter since they'd have had me on video surveillance arriving and leaving the stash house. Maybe they'd even been tailing me all the way from Ohio. Or tracking me for more than one trip just as they'd been surveilling the stash house. That they'd had the highway patrol, DEA, even the warehouse all waiting for me pointed to a carefully crafted ambush.

At this point I was too exhausted and in shock to care. The patrol officer drove me to a police precinct, where I was chained to a table in an interrogation room across from a couple DEA agents. They interrogated me for several hours, but I just repeated the same story I'd been instructed to give if I ever found myself in this situation. I was just a driver hired to take a vehicle from one place to another. I didn't know anything about drugs or false compartments. I didn't know about the people who'd hired me, much less those where I'd been paid to drop the car off. I was just doing my job.

Thankfully, I really didn't know much more than I'd admitted. But I did know my employers weren't the forgiving type and that I'd be putting my family in jeopardy if they thought I was snitching. It was a bit late to be thinking of my family now, but I was determined not to let my stupidity hurt my mom and brother. The agents eventually gave up pushing. Maybe because they'd already raided the stash house, as I know now, and had others in custody who could provide a lot more information than me.

By the time I was remanded over to booking, the sunrise was finally shining through the county jail windows. According to the paperwork, the official time I became a prisoner of the state of Oklahoma was 7:35 a.m. on July 24, 2006, just one month past my twenty-fifth birthday. I don't know exactly what the police officer in charge of booking saw when he looked at me. I was still wearing college casual—shorts, a tank-top, sandals—and I know I must have looked young, dog-tired, and scared, my head lowered in shame so I couldn't meet his gaze.

Gathering up my belongings to sack them, he picked up my California driver's license and shook his head, his expression both exasperated and compassionate. "You know, son, I'm from LA—Orange County. I've got a son just your age. What are you doing getting caught up in something like this? I'm so disappointed in you. You're better than this!"

This man didn't even know me, but he talked like a concerned father. Not my father who'd abandoned me, but a loving father like Oscar or Ken Mendoza. And I knew he was right. I felt sick with disappointment in myself.

> "I'm so thankful our Father God doesn't judge us as we judge others." —Abe Cruz

And his concern didn't stop there. After changing into an orange county jail jumpsuit, I was led to the holding area. The large cage-like cells held at least fifteen to twenty other prisoners, all much older and looking like seasoned convicts, many clearly drunk or high on meth or some other drug. With my Taekwondo training and being a former college athlete, I was no weakling. But the officer again shook his head sympathetically as he led me to a completely empty cell. "You don't need any more trouble, son, so let's keep you separate and avoid any issues."

Catching the angry glares and muttered curses from the other inmates, I knew what a blessing I'd just been handed. The cell had a phone for collect calls. The first thing I did was call that Beverly Hills phone number I'd been given in case I ever needed a lawyer. I sure needed one now!

But I got no answer. I must have dialed the number at least twenty-five times without an answer, and I was getting frustrated as well as panicked. How could an attorney's office not answer their phone? It didn't occur to me that with Oklahoma being two time zones ahead of LA, maybe the office wasn't open yet.

Finally, I gave up and called a number I hadn't wanted to call—my younger brother David. He had no idea what I'd been doing these last months. In his eyes I was a successful entrepreneur. How could I admit I'd been arrested—and why? As for Mom, I couldn't face the thought of telling her.

Unlike the attorney, David answered immediately. He knew it had to be trouble for me to be calling collect at that early hour. I quickly reassured him, "Hey brother, I'm fine. Don't panic. I'm in the county jail in Oklahoma City. But it's going to be okay. I just need you to get some of my cash, fly out here, and bail me out."

I gave him instructions to go to Mom's apartment and look behind the TV. There he'd find a brown paper bag with $30,000—my remaining stash from all the cash payments I'd been getting.

"Take the cash and my Beemer to the airport, buy yourself a ticket, and bring the rest with you."

However shocked he must have been, David didn't argue or cast blame or even ask where I'd gotten that kind of cash. "I'll be on the first flight I can get."

That settled, I made myself comfortable on the narrow bench that was all the cell offered for sitting and sleeping. There was no padding, but I'd been given a pillow and sheet, and by this time nothing could have kept me awake. I must have slept a full eight hours. When I awoke, I was served a bologna sandwich. From then on, there was nothing to do but sit and stare at the wall.

It took a couple days before David was able to arrange a flight to Oklahoma City and deal with my bail. I'll never forget the wonderful feeling when the guard came up to my cell and called out, "Cruz, you made bail."

The same booking officer gave me back all the belongings that had been confiscated. David was waiting for me outside. I hugged my brother, grateful he'd come to my rescue. It felt like this should be the end of my ordeal. That we could now go home and forget this nightmare.

But of course it was just beginning.

CHAPTER NINETEEN
GUILTY AS CHARGED

THE WORST WAS CALLING MOM. WHEN he'd picked up my cash, David had given her a story that I was off with some girl. But I'd now been gone six days, and I knew she had to be worried sick. And sooner or later, she'd have to find out. With my belongings returned, I now had my cell phone again. So as soon as David and I checked into a hotel for the night, I pulled out my phone.

I felt sick and shaky as I called her number. All my life, Mom had drilled into me to be a righteous, GOD-fearing, moral person. Even when she hadn't understood what I did, she'd been proud of my accomplishments as an athlete and business entrepreneur. When disaster struck, she'd always been there for me. Now I was going to have to destroy her image of her first-born. I wanted to cry just thinking of her disappointment. This was a hundred times worse than having to come for me because I'd been caught shoplifting.

But nothing I imagined was as bad as what actually happened. The moment Mom answered the phone, she cried out with anguish, "*M'ijo*, what have you done? The DEA is here raiding my house!"

In low, rapid Spanish, she went on to tell me there were at least two dozen agents with guns and dogs in the apartment. They were turning everything upside-down, even ripping out cupboards looking for drugs and cash. They hadn't found anything, thankfully, since I'd had David retrieve my brown bag of cash and I'd never been so stupid as to touch drugs. But the agents had confiscated my Rolex.

"They said it was bought with dirty money, so they took it!"

It broke my heart to hear Mom crying as she spoke. Then suddenly she broke off, and a man's voice came on her line. He identified himself as DEA, then began cursing me out, telling me I was a good-for-nothing son to be putting my mom through all this. "Where's the money, you piece-of-crap? Where's the cocaine?"

I didn't answer or argue, especially since I was in full agreement that I'd been a terrible son. Hearing my mom's terrified sobs in the background, I was even more determined to get home as soon as possible. But first I needed to find a local Oklahoma City criminal attorney to handle my case. After some research, David and I found one who took the case for a $25,000 retainer.

When we met with the attorney, he'd already checked out my case and let me know I had to be back in thirty days for my next court appearance. He seemed optimistic about my prospects. "You've got a clean record—no priors. And we can argue lack of probable cause for pulling you over. I think there's a good chance of getting you probation with no prison time."

Since my bail had been set at $120,000, I'd already had to pay $12,000 upfront to the bail bondsman. With the attorney's fee, my $30,000 in cash was more than wiped out. I was once again as dead-broke as when I'd taken that long step over the line to accept this job. At the moment, that was the least of my worries. I just wanted to go home and make things right for my mom.

David and I caught a flight to Hollywood-Burbank Airport just west of Pasadena where David had left my Beemer. When we walked out to where he'd parked, we couldn't find the car. We searched the entire lot, clicking the remote to set off the Beemer's alarm, but heard nothing. A black-on-black BMW with crystal lights and super-dark limo tint windows was not a car you could miss. It simply wasn't there.

We finally took a taxi home. The apartment had been restored to semi-order when we stepped inside. Mom screamed and burst into tears when she saw me, calling me all kinds of names I absolutely deserved even while she repeatedly hugged and kissed me.

"*M'ijo*, what were you thinking?" she kept asking.

"I'm so sorry!" I kept answering. "I'm so sorry!"

I had one more conversation to get through that I dreaded even more than telling Mom. My boss was clearly following what had happened to me since he called as soon as I got back to LA. The good news was that I didn't have to convince him it wasn't my fault that I'd failed to deliver my cargo.

"You win some, you lose some," he shrugged off the loss. "We figure on losing a car here and there. That's why we've got lawyers. So long as you followed instructions and kept your mouth shut, everything will be just fine."

That's when it hit me just how big this operation must be and how small a piece I was in it. Far from being someone special in some exciting, daredevil, technically-illegal but harmless real-life video game, I was just one of who knew how many drivers to who knew how many locations. Just how many of those had eventually ended up in the "lose some" column? As with my former "upline" leader, I was expendable, useful only so long as I was making money for him.

I assured my boss I'd given up no information. He seemed to believe me, perhaps because he wouldn't be sitting there free and clear calling me if I had. But he added, "Just keep in mind we know where your family lives and where you work!"

I wasn't stupid. Just like when he'd hired me, I'd seen enough movies to interpret the code of unsaid words. If I kept quiet, my family would be safe. If I talked, who knew what might happen to Mom and my siblings. Thankfully, I never saw the man again—or anyone from that world. What happened to him and his operation or how much the DEA learned from their various raids and arrests, I was just as glad not to ever find out to this very day. A door had closed on that part of my life, and I never wanted to knock on it again.

I was an emotional wreck by the time I went to bed that night. Mom came into my bedroom. She was no longer angry, just sad.

> **"GOD will never put us in a situation without giving us the strength to handle it."** —Abe Cruz

"What's going to happen now?" she asked.

In tears, I explained that I'd have to return to Oklahoma City in thirty days and that I had no idea what kind of charges or sentence I might be facing. Giving me a hug, Mom assured me, "*M'ijo*, you'll have to accept the consequences of what you did. But don't worry. God will never put us in a situation without giving us the strength to handle it, and he will be with you. You just have to not lose faith."

Except I was the one who'd put myself into this situation, not God, so why should he care about me? I thought back to when Mom had benched me for being disrespectful. My wrong-doing this time was infinitely worse, and the consequences would be too. But when Mom put her arm around me and began praying, I prayed with her. It was the first time in years I'd genuinely cried out to God, and if my prayers were all about me and for God to please keep me from going to prison, it was a start.

The strangest thing about the following weeks was life as normal. None of my acquaintances in LA outside my family knew about the arrest, so I simply went back to work at the gym and real estate office. I even earned some sizeable real estate commissions, which helped with my lawyer fees. I returned to a fairly normal social life, though without funds I stayed away from the clubs.

I kept in contact with my Oklahoma lawyer, and he confirmed that the DEA had indeed impounded the Beemer under the RICO Act, which allowed for seizure of assets from anyone charged with drug trafficking, racketeering, or other kinds of organized crime.

"We can file to get it back," he told me. "But you'd have to show how and where the funds came from to purchase the vehicle. Or you can just cut your losses."

That was a no-brainer since I could neither show legitimate source of funding nor could I afford to continue making car payments. So once again I was without a vehicle.

The thirty days were up faster than it seemed possible. Mom flew with me back to Oklahoma City for the arraignment. Having been assured I could hope for probation, I was stunned and devastated when the Oklahoma City DA (district attorney) offered a thirty-year violent felony sentence.

Thirty years for a first-time offender? I quickly learned that Oklahoma had some of the toughest drug trafficking laws in the country, including serving a minimum 85% of a violent-offense sentence. I was only twenty-five now, which meant I'd be over fifty by the time I was eligible for parole.

My life is over! I told myself, truly panicked for the first time. It suddenly made sense why the DEA might have chosen to wait until I'd crossed the Oklahoma state line before springing their trap if they'd had me under surveillance since the Ohio stash house.

"They're just trying to scare you," my attorney was quick to reassure me. "They'd like to make an example of you. But we don't have to accept that sentence. That's just their first offer. I'm here to fight for you."

So if I didn't have money for a good criminal defense lawyer, I might be stuck with thirty years! His statement made me wonder how many young inmates with minimal charges were behind bars for life just because they didn't have a cash reserve like me. For the first time, I seriously considered running. I had family connections in Mexico, and my late employers had contacts in Latin America and the Caribbean. I'd been a reliable, trustworthy employee these past eighteen months. I had no doubt they'd be willing to help me relocate if I agreed to keep working for them.

For just an instant, I had an image of rising the ladder of success as I'd daydreamed during my cross-country drives. Of having that million bucks in the bank, a mansion, the playboy lifestyle. Maybe not in LA, but Mexico City, Caracas, Bogotá, or Buenos Aires all offered the good life.

But that thought didn't last long. I didn't want to go to prison, but neither did I want to be a fugitive for the rest of my life. I didn't want to go back to the narco-life I'd just left even if it meant wealth and pleasure. I'd made a lot of mistakes. But this was a line I just couldn't step over. For one, it would break my mom's heart. After all she'd poured into me, I couldn't betray her like that. Or all the others who'd poured themselves into my life—Oscar, Ken, coaches, teachers.

But more than that, I had a conviction my story wasn't meant to end like this before it had really even started. Somewhere out there was a plan for my life. A plan for a better Abe Cruz. No, SOMEONE out there had a plan for my life. If I hadn't believed it before when Oscar and Mom talked to me about God and faith, if I'd mistakenly believed I could make my own plans and had control of my own life, my recent prayer times with Mom had reminded me of who was really in control and was the only one who could turn my life around.

And like Mom had also told me, that meant accepting the consequences for my actions, whatever those turned out to be.

CHAPTER TWENTY
LET'S MAKE A DEAL

THAT DECISION NOT TO RUN BECAME A turning point for me. There were far worse times ahead and a lot more life-changing decisions I'd have to make. But once running was no longer an option, my thoughts were how I would get through the consequences and what kind of future I'd have on the other side instead of trying to escape punishment or recapture the out-of-control life I'd been living.

This is also when I really started praying. I'd been letting Mom pray over me, pouring out her fear and worries for me to GOD. Now we began really praying together morning and night. For the first time, I admitted to GOD that my own wrong choices had led me to this situation and asked forgiveness. I also asked forgiveness from Mom and David for putting them in this situation.

But it didn't stop there. Mom was always fierce in fighting for her sons, even in spiritual matters. She called up several prayer chains and asked them to pray for me. Pretty soon there were prayer warriors contacting me from all over the country to tell me they were praying for me or calling to pray with me on the phone. Mom had also started attending a neighborhood church, and I began attending with her.

I was still really scared. Especially when the next thirty days passed and my attorney told me the DA wasn't budging from thirty years violent felony. The case dragged on month after month. Which meant I had to keep finding more money for the attorney. Beyond the brown bag of cash, I had a bit of savings. That was now all gone. Mom cleaned out her own savings to help, which made me feel even worse.

After several months, my lawyer informed me the DA had agreed to drop the sentence recommendation to twenty-five years non-violent, which came with minimum time served of 33% instead of 85%. That would still be at least eight years, an incredibly long chunk of time for a twenty-five-year-old. Once again the temptation to run reared its head, but this time I didn't let it linger. I'd told God, my mom, and all those people praying for me that I'd take whatever consequences I was given, and I intended to follow through.

I'm thankful I made that decision because I had no idea running was less of an option than I'd thought. One day Mom came into the gym while I was working. She left almost immediately. When I got home that evening, Mom told me to sit down. Almost in a whisper, she said, "*M'ijo, necesitamos hablar* [son, we need to talk]."

Her quiet tone was so urgent I was alarmed. "What's going on? What's wrong?"

"We're being watched and followed," she said. "Remember the DEA agents who raided the house? I saw two of them at the gym today working out right next to you. And I saw another following me today. There could be bugs on our phones or even in this house. You must be careful, *m'ijo*!"

I shouldn't have been surprised. The DEA had clearly not given up on hoping I'd lead them to more information. In truth, I didn't care if they followed me or listened in as I was done with my old life and they were just wasting man-hours. But I'm sure glad I didn't try to leave the country as I've no doubt I'd have been arrested.

The back-and-forth between my attorney and the DA lasted a full year. During that time, my only assignment was to check in every thirty days and stay out of trouble, which I did. Every dollar I scraped up went to additional retainer for the attorney. He'd managed to get a lower sentencing recommendation of twenty years non-violent but felt we could do better.

Then in August 2007, my attorney called. "I've got a new offer. Twelve years non-violent, which means with good behavior you'll serve maybe four. I don't think we'll get better. You want me to take it or go to trial? Keep in mind if we go to trial and you lose, you may be back at serving the full thirty years. My advice is you take it."

I didn't argue with his advice. For one, I had no more money to keep fighting this, and I just knew in my heart this was it. Believe me when I tell you God's prayer warriors praying together in faith really can move mountains, as the Bible says! No, the prayers hadn't eliminated a prison sentence. But they'd prepared me for the journey I was about to take and what was yet to come. And four years was a long drop from the original thirty. Instead of being out by fifty, I'd be out by thirty. I had faith it would be even less than that.

> "God's prayer warriors praying together in faith really can move mountains!" —Abe Cruz

But that didn't mean I wasn't terrified. Mom and David flew with me to Oklahoma City. We checked into a hotel and spent my last free night together crying, praying, and hugging. After Mom had gone to her room and David was asleep, I got down on my knees and began praying on my own, tears pouring down my cheeks.

Oddly, the thought of slipping out of the room, downstairs, and going on the run didn't even cross my mind. I'd gotten into this mess because of my own selfish, careless, chaotic mindset. I'd been offered a fair deal, and I'd made my decision. Until I'd paid for what I'd done and came out on the other side, I could never move forward to a new life and future.

Still, the thought of walking into that courtroom and surrendering myself to an imprisonment infinitely worse than those few days in lockup had me terrified. Rolling over to look up at the dark ceiling, I cried out to God. *Padre en los cielos* [Father in heaven], *I'm so sorry! This is all my fault. Please help me go through with this! Help me hold onto my faith in there!*

Then it was morning. Bleary with lack of sleep, I "dressed for success" one last time, putting on a nice suit and tie to make a good impression in court. Mom, David, and I met up with the attorney outside the courtroom. The three of us stood there in the hall holding hands while Mom prayed over me, asking God to teach me a lesson through what was about to happen and to turn this mistake into my biggest blessing.

Then David hugged me, saying, "Brother, God's going to be with you in there, so just keep strong. It's going to be okay."

By this point I was calm, even peaceful. Whatever was going to happen was going to happen. My attorney put his hand on my shoulder. "We've got to go now, Abe. The judge is waiting."

He was smiling and sounded cheerful. But then he wasn't the one going to prison. He added encouragingly like a coach sending me onto the football field. "You're a strong young man, Abe. You'll do just fine."

Mom and David stayed standing at the back of the courtroom as my attorney and I walked down the aisle to take a seat at the defendant's table. From that point everything seemed to be in slow motion. We all rose as the judge, a woman, entered the courtroom and took her seat. She looked at the file in her hand and then at me, smiling.

"Mr. Cruz, I see you've been staying out of trouble. So I'll be dropping your plea deal to ten years non-violent with twenty-five years' probation. What do you have to say to that, Mr. Cruz?"

Ten years! At 33% served, that meant I could be out in just over three years. I felt so blessed. I was seeing answered prayer in action. All I could do was smile and stutter. "Wow! Thank you so much, your honor!"

I also thanked my attorney for all he'd done. With a smile, he assured me, "This isn't over yet. You stay out of trouble, do all programs you can, and at the end of a year I'll see what I can do to get you a judicial review. If all goes well, hopefully you won't have to serve more than a year."

Wow, again! I wasn't hearing "if," "hopefully," or "I'll see what I can do," but "you won't have to serve more than a year." I felt even more blessed and excited.

"Then you are now remanded by the state of Oklahoma to ten years in the Oklahoma Department of Corrections." The judge's gavel came down hard. "Take him away."

A bailiff came forward to put me in handcuffs. That was when I heard my mom cry out in anguish. Turning, I saw her fall to the floor at the back of the courtroom, sobbing inconsolably. My brother was trying to support her.

All my excitement for the lighter sentence evaporated. Seeing her grief and pain was the worse punishment of my ordeal to date, driving home like a knife into my heart just how stupid, selfish, and arrogant I'd been to bring such anguish and sorrow to the one person who'd done the most for me my whole life. All I could do was vow silently that I would somehow make it up to her.

Still in suit and tie, I was led back out of the courtroom to join four other prisoners in orange jumpsuits. This took me past my mom and brother. Struggling to compose herself, Mom came close enough to say quietly, "*M'ijo, no pierdas la fe.* [my son, don't lose faith]. *Dios tiene un plan y no te abandonará* [GOD has a plan and will not abandon you]."

David called out, "Stay strong, brother."

Then they were gone and a guard was directing me and the other prisoners into an elevator. Already, depression was closing in on me, and once again it felt that my life was over. Just then the guard, a stocky, middle-aged man, leaned over to say quietly, "*No te desmayes, hijo* [don't be discouraged, son]. *Todo estará bien* [all will be well]. *Dios está contigo* [GOD is with you]."

I was stunned at the guard's words. Who would have thought I'd find a Spanish-speaking guard here in Oklahoma, much less one who spoke of GOD with such conviction—and kindness! Perhaps he'd heard my mom's words so figured I came from a religious family. But it was as though GOD had leaned down to speak to me through that guard's compassionate remarks.

Suddenly I no longer felt so alone.

CHAPTER TWENTY-ONE
ROCK BOTTOM

WHEN WE EXITED THE ELEVATOR INTO booking, I was surprised to see behind the glass the same officer who had booked me a year earlier. He recognized me too. "Cruz, it's been awhile."

Once again, I had to turn in all my belongings and change my suit and tie for an orange prison jumpsuit. Handing me a jail bag with toothbrush, soap, a small tube of toothpaste, and other toiletries, the booking officer told me kindly, "Look, Cruz, you're a big guy. You can take care of yourself in there. Just be respectful, don't get into any arguments or fights, and you'll make it through this."

I appreciated his kindness, but my new reality was beginning to sink in as I was led into an open pod, as each inmate section was called. These were laid out in a circle with two tiers of forty cells each looking out onto an open central area with tables for meals and socializing. Peeling pea-green walls were covered with racial slurs and other graffiti. Each cell was meant for two men with narrow upper and lower bunks and a stainless-steel toilet, sink, and mirror. But the pod was so overcrowded most cells had three and four prisoners, the extras sleeping on thin mats on the concrete floor. We all shared just three shower stalls.

When I was led in, it was like walking into a zoo or battle zone. Clusters of prisoners divided mostly by ethnicity were all huddled in different areas, yelling and cursing at each other. The guards watched indifferently from behind large glass windows in an office area that overlooked the entire pod.

As I walked in, all eyes swiveled to stare at me, sizing me up. I'd continued training the whole year I was waiting for sentencing and was at my heaviest muscle mass ever—5'9" and 195 pounds—so I wasn't too worried about being challenged one-on-one. I walked by a Latino group, who stared me up and down until I spoke to them in Spanish.

"*¿De donde eres?* [where are you from?]," they asked me.

Once they found out I was a Latino from LA and had grown up in the hood, they had my back. With my Caucasian features, highlighted hair, light-skinned tan, and body-building physique, I looked like the stereotypical California Beach Boy. So the Caucasian prisoners assumed I was one of them too. And since I'd grown up in a predominantly African-American neighborhood and played on mostly African-American sports teams, I knew how to blend in there too. In fact, I never did have any real problems with any racial group while I was in there.

That was good because I found out the pod was on lockdown because of a race riot just a couple days earlier. It remained on lockdown the first three weeks I was there. I ended up in a cell with two other prisoners, an older man who was on Thorazine, a powerful sleep med/antidepressant that left him knocked out at least twenty hours a day, and a small, thin, quiet man who stayed to himself.

Since they had the bunks, I slept on the hard, cold concrete with just a mat under me. As I lay there awake, flashbacks of my life kept playing in my mind. I remembered all the good times, the thrill of being a winner on the football field and basketball court. But then the bad times would run through my mind. All the stupid, drunken waste of money at the clubs and casinos. The terror of that knife attack. The DEA ambush. The grief and pain and disappointment on my mom's face.

I kept reminding myself of Mom's words. *God is with you. You aren't alone.* But I felt miserably depressed. Because of the rioting, we weren't allowed out in the common area. Our meals were passed into the cells on trays. These consisted of oatmeal or grits for breakfast, a bologna sandwich at lunch, then macaroni-and-cheese, pasta with ground meat, or some other starch for supper.

The servings were small, and with my muscle mass I burned a lot of calories, so I was always hungry.

But that was nothing compared to the thirst. For the first three days we had water. Then the sink in our cell stopped working. The only liquids we had were what came with meals. I let the guards know over and over that we had no water, but they just ignored our request. Finally one day I was trying to do some of my normal fitness routine when I passed out from dehydration.

It was the best thing that could have happened to me. I was sent to the infirmary where two nice female nurses gave me eight cups of deliciously cold water. When they asked why I was so dehydrated, I explained about the broken sink. It was immediately repaired.

But that wasn't my only health issue. For the past year I'd been taking steroids. Turning myself in meant quitting cold turkey, which caused all kinds of side effects, including a return of severe acne all over my face, shoulders, and back. When I requested medical treatment, they told me my issues were cosmetic, not life-threatening, so I was denied medication. Once again, I could no longer stand to look at myself in the mirror.

There were other things that to me seemed clear injustice and abuse of power by the guards. One issue involved my mail. Mom had been writing me along with some of her prayer warriors. So had a number of girls I'd partied with in the clubs. The guards had to open all mail and were enjoying some of the provocative pictures the girls had included.

When I asked for my mail, the guards kept giving me excuses. I finally lost it. We'd been locked back in our cells. I was so furious I began kicking at the locked cell door until it suddenly burst open. That brought me to my senses. I picked the door up and put it back on its hinges.

Not long after, the guards brought me my mail. Though they saw the broken door, they didn't say anything or even write me up. They just moved me to another cell. But they also didn't withhold my mail again.

I was originally supposed to be in county jail for just thirty to sixty days before being transported to Lexington, the big central prison where prisoners were assessed according to crimes and given their long-term assignment to different prisons across the state. I ended up being there four months. At least the lockdown had ended, so we were allowed to leave our cells and mingle in the common area.

But that created another danger since more than two hundred prisoners were now milling around loose with the guards remaining at a safe distance behind their windows. I turned to my usual default no matter what life threw at me—physical training. But how do you do that in a prison pod with no gym equipment?

I ended up turning the underside of an open staircase leading to the second level of cells into a workout station. A metal step an arms-length above my head became a pull-up bar. The concrete floor was my push-up mat. The steps themselves were a stair-master.

When I was moved to my new cell, I acquired a new roommate who was a member of the Crips, a major LA street gang. Like me, he'd been an LA high school athlete. Once we discovered we had some acquaintances in common, he became quite friendly. Fascinated by my creative jail training regimen, he began joining me in workouts.

One day when I started my routine out in the pod, I noticed two Crips walk up on me. Both were smaller than me, maybe 5'6" and 150 lbs., their entire upper bodies and faces covered with tattoos. They began circling me like a pair of wolves, one glaring coldly into my eyes while the other would edge around to my backside.

I shifted to try to keep both of them in my line of sight. The entire pod had fallen quiet, watching. I'd never felt in such danger of my life even when that knife came at me at the Waffle House. I was fairly confident I could defend myself one-on-one, but I wasn't so sure if both came at me together.

Fists balled, I'd braced myself for their rush when my cell-mate's powerful voice suddenly screamed out, "Leave Cruz alone! He's cool."

The speed with which those two Crips backed off made clear who was boss-man in that pod. I had no more trouble in my remaining months there. In fact, that encounter turned out to be the scariest moment of my time in prison. Like the guard who'd spoken to me in Spanish and the booking officer, my new cellmate turned out to be a real blessing God sent me in that place, and I told him so.

I was dead asleep in the middle of the night when a guard came to my cell and called out, "Wake up, Cruz. Pack your bags. You're leaving."

My transfer to Lexington Assessment and Reception Center, Oklahoma's male intake facility, had finally come through. I was just there a short time while awaiting my long-term assignment. One significant thing happened there. I found a book in my cell called *The Purpose Driven Life* by a Christian pastor named Rick Warren.

Though I'd never been much on academics, I'd started to read when I was given leadership books at those business presentations back in college. But I'd never read a religious book except the Bible—and that only for religion classes at Catholic school. This book asked the very question I'd been asking—what on earth am I here for?—and talked about how to understand God's purpose for your life. Since a new purpose and future was exactly what I needed, Rick Warren's words had a big impact on me—and still do.

Every day I prayed for God's direction for my future. I'd seen God's hand on all the blessings and protection I'd received so far. So it was a great shock when I received my assignment. "Cruz, you're headed to Dick Conner's."

> "You can't just ask God to take away all your problems or give you everything you want. You need to first ask God what his plans are to make you the best you can be." —Abe Cruz

Holding about twelve hundred male prisoners, Dick Conner Correction Facility in Osage County about two hours north of

Oklahoma City, was designated specifically for violent offenders. Notorious for racial feuding and violence, it averaged at least one stabbing a week and murder per month. I was in for a non-violent offense, so I couldn't understand why I'd been assigned there.

Shackled wrists and ankles, I was loaded on a bus with other prisoners headed to DCCF. Some had been there before and took pleasure in telling me of the stabbings, beatings, and killings they'd witnessed and what fresh meat like me could expect. I can admit I was terrified as we pulled into the DCCF unloading zone.

A guard stepped onto the bus. Then to my surprise, he called out my name. "Abe Cruz, you stay seated."

He added, "The rest of you, this is your stop. Welcome to Dick Conner Correctional Facility."

Once the other prisoners were unloaded, the guard walked me over to a small white van lettered with the words Creek County Jail, Sapulpa, Oklahoma. As I climbed inside, the driver told me, "You're a lucky kid, Cruz! Dick Conner's is already at maximum capacity, so you're being sent to overflow. You don't want to be at Conner's anyway. A kid like you would get pushed into doing something you didn't want and find yourself catching more time. You're going to like Creek County a whole lot better."

I knew it wasn't luck. Once again, God had intervened to bless and protect me. And the driver was right about Creek County. The pod where I found myself was much smaller—just twenty-two cells and forty-four prisoners. Nor were these violent offenders. The majority were there for drug use and petty crimes committed to fuel their habit. Now that they were clean, they were fairly decent, ordinary men just trying to do their time and stay out of trouble. A lot of them were on Thorazine, so they slept much of the time.

By now I was four months into my sentence. In truth, I no longer thought about the original ten-year sentence or 33% guidelines that would mean serving at least three years. I'd become convinced the one-year review my attorney had promised was God's plan to get me out of here, and I'd staked all my hopes on that. The review was still eight months away, but I figured the easiest way to get through this was to follow my pod-mates' lead and just sleep away the rest of the year.

Getting a prescription for Thorazine was easy. I just had to tell the truth—that I felt sad and depressed. I basically ate my meals and slept for the next four months. Now I had only four months left. I figured I could do that standing on my head. Then a letter from my attorney brought my comfortable cocoon crashing down.

"I'm sorry to inform you that your judicial review has been denied," he wrote. "The DA doesn't feel a one-year punishment is enough time for you to learn your lesson."

I was crushed. All these months I'd kept out of trouble and done everything asked of me with the expectation of that one-year review. If I'd felt depressed before, I was now in a freefall of confusion, misery, fear, and anger. How could I even wrap my mind around another two to three years or more behind bars? How could I tell Mom? She too had been counting on that one-year review.

For the next few days I just huddled on my bed crying. None of my pod-mates paid any attention. They were too buried in their own troubles and Thorazine haze. After all my hopes and prayers for a new beginning, my life was a total failure. And I'd lost all faith it could ever be any different.

Thank GOD I was once again totally wrong!

CHAPTER TWENTY-TWO
PRAYER AND FASTING

SO WHAT WAS I TO DO NOW? I'D PLANNED to just sleep through a few more months of incarceration. But I couldn't sleep for the next three years or more. If prison was to be my long-term reality, I needed to do something with my life *now*, not just plan on waiting until I got out. I finally made myself call Mom, but I was too choked-up to speak.

"*M'ijo*, what's wrong?" she asked worriedly.

I finally got the words out. "Mom, I received a letter from my attorney. He said the DA denied my one-year judicial review. I don't know when I'll be out. It could be years!"

After her reaction in the courtroom, I was worried Mom would completely lose it at this news. So I was dumbfounded when instead she said calmly, "*M'ijo*, everyone goes to GOD when they're in trouble or want something, expecting GOD to just give them whatever they ask for. But they don't want to have to sacrifice anything themselves or make any changes.

"That includes you, Abraham. GOD is the only one who can give you a second chance. He is the only one who can show you light for this journey through the darkness. If you really want GOD to give you a second chance at life, you need to pray to him and tell him how sorry you are for everything you've done. You need to *show* him you are willing to sacrifice for GOD."

She was right, I knew. Mom always was when she spoke about GOD and faith. It was like a lightbulb suddenly went off in my head as I realized how self-centered and childish my prayers had been. I'd never expected to win on the football field or basketball court without sacrificing. How many years of time, hard work, and constant practice had I invested? And that was just to win a game! How could I even have thought of offering GOD less?

"But what can I do in a prison cell?" I asked. "How can I sacrifice to GOD in here?"

"In the Bible when people wanted to hear from GOD, they prayed and fasted," Mom answered. "Jesus prayed and fasted for forty days and nights in the wilderness before he began his public ministry here on earth. Moses fasted for forty days and nights on the mountain before GOD gave him the Ten Commandments. The Bible speaks of many other fasts when people were seeking answers from GOD. In fact, Jesus told his disciples that some miracles only come about through prayer and fasting. Faith alone isn't enough."

She went on firmly, "*M'ijo*, you need to show GOD you are willing to sacrifice for him by praying and fasting for forty days. Just one meal a day and some water. GOD will hear your prayers and grant you a second opportunity at life. This is the only way, *m'ijo*. You must do it!"

I could hear her passionate concern for me in her voice. By the end of the call, we were both crying together on the phone, but I had promised to do as she asked. I started that same evening, kneeling beside the narrow shelf-like bunk that was my bed. I paid no attention to the stares of other pod-mates who could see me. Silently, I opened my heart and just talked to GOD as I'd heard Mom do so many times..

Dear Father GOD, I am so messed up. I am so sorry for neglecting you and not listening and not living your way these past twenty-six years. I've made so many excuses. I haven't taken responsibility for my choices. I've hurt other people through my selfish actions. So this what I'm going to do. I'm going to fast for you, sacrifice for you, for the next forty days to show how serious I am. If I do this, won't you please give me a second chance? Won't you please let me get back into the outside world sooner than later? If you get me out of here, I promise I will represent you in everything I do. I will do everything I can to help your world become a better place. To help those who are less fortunate.

I'll admit I was still acting pretty immature, bargaining with God like some game of Let's Make a Deal. I'm so thankful our Father God doesn't judge us as we judge others. That he knows when we are sincerely repentant and has mercy on us even when we still don't have it all together. Maybe my prayer was far from perfect, but it was totally sincere.

That night as I slept, I began having incredibly descriptive, powerful dreams such as I'd never had. There were bright, vivid images like I was reliving Bible stories and human history—Adam and Eve in the Garden of Eden, dinosaurs roaming, God creating trees and plants and animals, events like Moses freeing the Israelites or David fighting Goliath that I didn't even realize then were stories out of the Bible.

One of those visions was of the Old Testament patriarch Abraham, for whom I was named, standing on a hill overlooking a vast land, while God said to him, "Because of your faith and obedience to me, I am going to bless you and you are going to be a blessing to others. People all over the earth will be blessed because of you."

I had no idea until much later that this vision was right out of the Bible (Genesis 12:18, Galatians 3:9). Nor did I realize then that it was a prophecy of my own future. Of God's great blessing on my life. Of God allowing me to be a blessing to others in many different parts of the world.

The most incredible part of this vision was that I *knew* God was there with me. I don't have words to describe the experience, as though light and warmth and love were being injected straight into me. But it felt like I was being hugged by a tender, caring father—the kind of father I'd never had—who was wiping away my tears and saying just like my mom does, "*M'ijo, te amo!* [my son, I love you!]"

I recognized then that in all the years I'd been angry for being fatherless, for a childhood of poverty and pain and rejection, for everything that had gone wrong and my feelings that God had let me down, that in fact, my heavenly Father had never left me. He'd sent me blessings that far outweighed the hard times. He'd given me a mom who loved me and fought for me and never gave up on me. He'd shown me fatherly love through mentors like Ken Mendoza, Oscar, coaches who cared about me, even police officers who'd expressed concern and compassion. And he was with me right here in this dark, depressing prison.

When I woke up the next morning, I felt clean and brand-new. I immediately began planning my forty-day fast. I spent the day hours fasting from both food and water, then would have a single meal and water in the evening. Mom had told me I could expect to feel weak from the fast, but in fact I felt strong and more alert than I had in years.

I started each day with a time of prayer, thanking God for all his blessings and everything he was doing for me in here. Then I'd spend the rest of the day writing letters to Mom and David, socializing with other inmates, playing card games, as well as reading the Bible and books from the prison library.

I gave my breakfast and lunch trays to other inmates, eating only the evening meal. Before touching that, I'd do a full training session, following the routine I'd come up with back at Oklahoma City County Jail. I was losing a lot of weight. In fact, I lost almost thirty pounds in this period. But I felt stronger and fitter than ever before. I would finish my day with another time of prayer.

Every night I also experienced new dreams. They were so vivid and clear, even after waking up, that I knew they were visions from God. I saw myself looking out over great crowds just as Abraham had looked out over the land God promised him. I saw myself helping people of all ages and talking to them about how much God loved them. There were children who'd hurt themselves. Teens in juvenile detention. An old man who'd fallen down and needed picked up.

> "I'd never expected to win on the football field or basketball court without sacrificing time, hard work, and constant practice. How could I think of offering God less?" —Abe Cruz

Over the weeks of my fast, I began to notice that the core theme of all these visions was of me doing things to serve other people. It brought to mind a quote I'd read from motivational speaker Jim Rohn: "The greatest service to mankind is finding a way to serve many people." Taking this to the next level, I recognized that the greatest way to serve GOD was serving other people. This was true sacrifice for GOD. This was the future to which GOD was calling me.

I saw other things too I knew were glimpses GOD was giving me of the future. I saw my face on magazine covers. I saw myself writing books, inspirational comics, movie scripts. I saw myself using my interest in clothing design and fitness to develop an inspirational fitness program and a faith-based clothing line. I saw myself on TV and speaking to millions all over the world. I knew in my visions that this was the second chance I'd asked GOD for, my new beginning in life.

My old self would have seen this as one more ladder to success, fortune, and glory. This time I knew that none of what I saw was about me accomplishing anything or becoming rich and famous. This was about serving others, bringing glory to GOD, and bringing GOD's love to other people. It was about using the platform GOD gave me to show people how faithful GOD is when we show how faithful we are to him.

Every day when I got up, I wrote down these visions. I made lists of what I'd seen in the future—speaking engagements, covers of magazines, TV, film, companies I would own, writing a book. I sketched out ideas for my comic book series and movie script. Both of these were about a young protagonist called Dark Justice who is GOD's warrior on a mission to uncover his father's murder and bring justice at whatever cost. The plot line was filled with my own experiences with drug trafficking, corruption, and illicit money.

One of my pod-mates, a big guy who stood at least 6'4" and weighed over three hundred pounds, was a talented artist. He earned money for commissary by creating cards prisoners could send home to their families. He wanted to get in shape, so I began trading training services for help on the comic book. I would lay out my ideas for plotlines and dialogue, and he would draw them.

I also wrote down inspirational thoughts God gave me. One scribbled note says, "I will be on the cover of magazines all over the world to inspire and motivate people in difficult and challenging situations!" Another reads, "God's truth uncovers Satan's lies." A third: "Dreams are simply goals not yet met."

Or slogans for my envisioned clothing line: "No Sacrifice, No Victory! . . . Heart over Mind . . . Train by Faith, Not by Sight . . . The Impossible Becomes Possible with Faith."

I still have all the papers I scribbled on in prison. What is really mind-blowing is that everything I saw in those visions has come true. More about that later. Of course I had no idea then how far into my future any of this might happen. But I was no longer in a hurry to get out of prison. That DA had said a year wasn't long enough for me to learn my lesson, and it was clear God agreed with him. I now understood that God was using my prison experience as a training camp in patience, humility, understanding, and growing in faith. Whatever God's plans for my future, they would come to fruition in his good time.

As to my new beginning, that wasn't for after getting out of prison.

That was now!

CHAPTER TWENTY-THREE
NEW BEGINNING

NONE OF THIS WAS HAPPENING IN A VACUUM. Other prisoners started asking me what I was doing. I would share why I was fasting and what GOD was doing in my life. Several inmates asked to join my training sessions. I eventually had about eight guys working out with me.

And not just physical training. We'd work out and eat our evening meal. Then I'd hold meetings like I'd done with my teammates and other college students during my business venture days. But instead of talking about how to make money, we'd read the Bible, leadership books, even fitness magazines like *Iron Man*.

Weight training was our biggest challenge since prisoners weren't permitted anything that could be used as a weapon. We started collecting plastic bags, which we'd layer inside each other, then fill with water. Grocery-sized bags worked for ten-pound weights while trash-can liners could hold up to a hundred pounds. Wooden rods from toilet plungers and brooms became handles from which to hang our water-balloon weights.

I'd been serious about working out clear back to working out in front of the TV as a kid. Now I took the time to really educate myself on physical training and nutrition. Truth is, out there in the real world we're often moving so fast and are so distracted by the chaos of life that we overlook the potential with which GOD has gifted us. All this time on my hands in prison allowed me to slow down and really focus on becoming the best me I could become.

How we ended up with a subscription to *Iron Man* is a story in itself. I've mentioned *NPC West Coast Classic* host Lonnie Teper, who got me started on bodybuilding. While I was in prison, a friend from LA, Joe Shen, entered the same competition. Jay Cutler, a four-times Mr. Olympia (the ultimate bodybuilding award) was a guest celebrity for the event. Joe got him to write me a personal autograph that read, "Hurry up and get out of prison. Once you're out, train hard!" It was signed "Jay Cutler, Mr. O."

Wow! I don't know what lifted me up more—a personalized autograph from one of the greatest bodybuilders of all time or a friend like Joe who would go to so much effort for me. Joe also sent me a twelve-month subscription to *Iron Man* Magazine. I read each issue with my group, learning about the right foods to eat, the best times for weight loss and muscle growth, and other valuable information on fitness.

Besides the Bible, I was reading a lot of leadership and self-development books. One book I read was *The 21 Irrefutable Laws of Leadership* by a Christian author named John C. Maxwell. I was surprised and impressed to find out how many principles of good leadership I'd learned were right out of the Bible. Motivational speaker Jim Rohn also referenced "the Good Book" (Bible) in his leadership principles.

Their teaching made me realize that being a good leader wasn't about becoming successful, wealthy, or famous. After all, Jesus is the greatest leader of all time, and he taught that those who want to be first need to serve others. That's how Jesus lived his own life. Treating others as you want to be treated, being kind, respectful, loving, caring—those were the characteristics of a true leader I'd encountered in Oscar and other mentors. That was the kind of leader I wanted to be. That was the mindset of a true champion.

About this time I met another true champion who has impacted my life ever since. Creek County Jail had a prison ministry sponsored by several Sapulpa-area churches. A lot of good people volunteered, but to be honest I have little memory of them. They typically stayed out in the main common area and invited anyone interested to join them for a religious service.

I can't blame them for being nervous about walking alone into a large group of convicted felons. But that made John Helstrom really stand out. A stocky, gray-haired man in his late sixties, he would walk right into our pod without hesitation or fear. I will never forget our first encounter. I was scribbling my usual notes while watching TV when he walked over and laid a hand on my shoulder.

"What's your name, young man?" he asked.

His smile was contagious so I smiled back. "I'm Abraham Cruz. Abe is what they call me."

"Abraham—that's a name out of the Bible. Abraham was a man of faith. A great reminder that God loves you and wants you to have a future. So how are you doing, Abe? Tell me about yourself. How are you holding up in here?"

> **"The core characteristics of a true leader are loving God and loving others."** —Abe Cruz

Lovingkindness just oozed out of John, and he always seemed genuinely interested in me and my pod-mates. After he made the rounds of the pod, he'd grab a Bible and start talking about what it said. He didn't care what religious or ethnic background we came from any more than that we were convicted felons. Protestants, Catholics, Muslims, Jews, agnostics, every possible racial mix—we were all brothers reading the Good Book and praying together.

John told stories of people in the Bible who'd made big mistakes, but God had forgiven them and turned their lives around. King David and the apostle Paul are two I remember well. John's takeaway was always that God loved us and that we had a future. He also talked about Jesus and how Jesus sacrificed himself for us on the cross so we could be forgiven and have hope of a future. Not just here in prison or after we got back into the outside world, but forever in heaven.

A lot of what John said about Jesus I'd heard before in Catholic school. But back then it was head knowledge to be repeated on a test for religion class. Now it became heart knowledge. Everything started fitting into place and making sense for the first time. I felt brand-new inside like I really had started all over with a new beginning. I know now this was the Holy Spirit working in my heart and life.

I also came to realize how simple the Bible's message really is. We make it so complicated with all our discussions of theology and doctrine. But Jesus himself when asked about the greatest of God's commandments summed up in just two sentences what faith is really all about (Luke 10:27). Love the Lord your God with all your heart, soul, strength, and mind. Love your neighbor as yourself. In other words, the same core principles that define the mindset of a champion—put God first and serving others second!

The rest of the Bible is filled with stories of God's power and miracles. Of mistakes we humans have made. Of decisions good and bad. Of teachings that would keep our lives smooth-sailing if we'd just do what they said. Of people who chose to follow God and people who chose to reject him. But in the end it boils down to the same basic principles that mark a true leader—loving God and loving others.

Things weren't always so upbeat in our pod. We had four phones available, and every few days I would call Mom. I knew she was struggling to get by without me helping her at all financially. But she spent all our time together lifting my spirits and encouraging me to trust God.

Other inmates didn't have someone like her in their lives. It was impossible not to overhear their phone conversations. I'd hear husbands blaming their wives for their problems or fathers yelling at their children. Others were in despair that their families had abandoned them. These were big, tough guys, but they'd break down in tears, saying, "What am I going to do when I get out? I have nothing. No one. At least here I have a bed to sleep in, three meals a day, and a shower. I'd rather just stay inside!"

There was violence too. Racial conflict between inmates flared up on a regular basis. The worst incident was a young man, maybe twenty years old, who was just a few months from release. He joined my evening group and would listen while we read and discussed different topics, though he was mainly interested in the fitness workouts. I knew he'd had a difficult life, so I tried to share God's love in a way he would accept.

Then one day he got into a quarrel with another inmate who owed him fifty cents for a Ramen noodle packet. When the other inmate didn't pay, the young man stabbed him in the neck with a sharpened pencil. Instead of being a few months from freedom, he was taken away and given a long additional sentence.

The worst was that these guys weren't just giving up on themselves. They were giving up on their families. Their children. Having grown up having a father who'd given up on being one, it hurt my heart to see fathers give up on making any kind of future with their children. I would try to share with them that God loves all of us. That he wants to give us a second chance. But you can't push your thoughts and beliefs on others who aren't ready to hear. It's like another powerful quote I'd learned, this one from President Teddy Roosevelt who said, "People don't care how much you know until they know how much you care."

That means you can't just walk up to someone who is hurting and tell them that everything will be fine if they'd just get their act together. You have to take time to get to know them where they are. You have to show them what God's love means. Show that you care about them. In other words, be to others what John Helstrom had been to me.

"Don't lose faith. God loves you," I'd say. "Okay, so maybe you aren't ready to believe in God. Then have faith in yourself. Have faith that you can have a future. Have faith that things will work out. When you lose faith, it's over. So if nothing else, keep your faith alive."

One day I was playing a game of spades with some pod-mates while a nearby TV screen aired the reality show, "I Want To Work For Diddy." The show featured a competition to become the next personal assistant to Sean John Combs, a famous rapper and clothing designer. To win, the contestants had to come up with a viable business plan to take the Sean John fashion brand to the next level.

As we played, I began sharing the vision God had given me of starting a fashion brand that would inspire and motivate people, not just because some celebrity was wearing it but because of its message and purpose. After all, everyone wears clothes, so it's a product that always has a market. Except I wouldn't be doing it for fame and profit but to help others. To change people's lives. To impact the world.

The other card players laughed at me and told me I was crazy. Like a convicted felon had the chance of a snowman in a volcano at becoming a successful business entrepreneur! I just ignored their jibes and began throwing out ideas for naming my brand.

Then suddenly it hit me. All God had shown me in my visions about faith. All the times Mom had told me, "Don't lose faith, *m'ijo*." All the times I'd encouraged my pod-mates to keep the faith. Faith isn't sometimes. Faith isn't maybe it'll work out. Or I sure hope it's true. Faith is real. Faith is forever.

And with that I knew I had my brand and my message—Forever Faith.

CHAPTER TWENTY-FOUR
KEEPING THE FAITH

FROM THAT POINT ON, I BEGAN CREATING what I call to this day my business plan from prison. Over the following months, I jotted down every thought and image that came to mind. Designs for clothing, jewelry, dog-tags. Slogans and inspirational sayings. Choices of color and fabric. I realized I'd been preparing for this since I'd started creating my own fashion style clear back in elementary school.

My artist friend helped me draw logos and clothing patterns. We created lines for every age, even onesies for infants. *Forever Faith* became my signature to everything I did. I would even write it on the outside of envelopes when I sent letters to my mom, brother, and other friends.

I eventually showed John Helstrom all my ideas. I just wanted to know if my scribblings had value to anyone besides myself. John's response was encouraging. "These are incredible. As to whether your visions will come to be, GOD is in the business of working miracles. He did miracles for your namesake Abraham. If this is GOD's future for you, he can certainly make it happen."

John ended up telling me, "Look, son, GOD has something special for you. When you get out of here, I want you to call me. Anything you need, just look me up."

I'd originally come to Creek County as overflow and had expected to be moved within a few months to a long-term facility. I am thankful now I was left there a full thirteen months before receiving my new assignment. Like Dick Conner's, James Crabtree Correctional Center (JCCC) was a medium security prison of about twelve hundred inmates and intended for violent offenders, which I was not.

Upon arrival, my assigned counselor informed me, "Mr. Cruz, you're not supposed to be at this facility, but we're overcapacity to move you elsewhere. We'll do our best to get you out of here, but it could be three to six months."

As we finished my orientation meeting, she added, "Just be careful and watch your back."

Not exactly comforting advice! By then I wasn't surprised about the overcapacity problem. At that time, Oklahoma had the highest per capita incarceration rate in the world and has been alternating since with Louisiana. Yes, that's right! Not in the United States or North America, but on the entire planet. Almost four times that of Iran. Ten times that of China. My new pod had around two hundred inmates, many of them lifers with no motivation to stay out of trouble or fighting.

There was no John Helstrom here. Nor any programs or jobs due to the maxed-out capacity. But I was no longer a scared new inmate. At least this place had an indoor basketball court and running track, so I spent a lot of time running, working out, and continuing my own reading program. Otherwise I kept to myself.

About four months later, a guard once again woke me up in the middle of the night. "Cruz, you're being transferred!"

My first thought was relief. I'd actually made it through this place without a scratch. *Thank you, Father GOD!*

My new assignment turned out to be Frederick Community Work Center in Frederick, OK, a couple hours southwest of Oklahoma City. I was excited about the move as a work center assignment typically indicates release isn't too far away. I'd been in now for almost two years. I could do another year or two easy if I had the assurance I'd soon be free.

And FCWC was a Boy Scout camp compared to Crabtree. With only a hundred or so prisoners, accommodation were far more comfortable, including separate toilets and showers that actually had warm water. The food was the best I'd eaten in two years. Since the facility was minimum security, there weren't even any fences. There was also a gym, softball field, and real weights.

Even better, a work center meant being assigned a job instead of sitting around all day. Which is where I again talked myself into trouble. Not long before, I'd finally been prescribed a medication for my acne problem that left the skin extremely sensitive if exposed to the sun. My first morning at Frederick, I was assigned to cleaning streets. With temperatures over a hundred degrees Fahrenheit, my face was bright-red and blistered by evening.

I explained my problem to my work-detail officer. I probably shouldn't have mentioned that I needed to take care of my face because I expected to be on TV and magazine covers once I got out of prison. The guard was not sympathetic. "Cruz, you just get out there, shut up, and do your job. If you don't shape up, you can count on being shipped back to a violent offender facility."

I shut up and shaped up since I sure didn't want to go back to Crabtree. Thankfully, it was only about a week before I received a new assignment, though by then my face and other exposed skin was badly burnt and peeling. My new job involved organizing and distributing inmate clothing. I was finished by three p.m., so I had the rest of the afternoon to work out. What a difference real weights were from water bags and broomsticks. With release in sight, I focused on improving my physique to be ready for those magazine covers.

GOD answered another prayer when I was transferred to work at the Frederick town hospital, doing prep work in the kitchen. Perks included incredible food such as chicken, fish, steak, as well as all the protein shakes I wanted. In other words, a perfect fitness diet. My strength and level of fitness were now back to what they'd been before prison, and I was the happiest I'd been in years.

I still had no friends to train or study with like I'd had at Creek County, in part because this facility offered so many other activities and programs along with a full workday. But I made good friends with fellow inmates and even the guards and warden. They all thought I was crazy when I talked about my future. But they also cheered me on, and I could see they wanted my dreams to come true even if they figured it wasn't possible for an ex-con.

> "Dreams are simply goals not yet met."
>
> —Abe Cruz

Then one day my counselor told me, "Cruz, time to get your driver's license."

I knew what that meant because you didn't need ID or a license until you were released. The counselor warned me that my release could still be several months ahead and would depend on my continued good behavior. Then she asked, "So what are your plans once you leave? You realize you'll still be on probation so you can't leave the state of Oklahoma."

I hadn't even thought of the immediate future—only the long-term future I'd seen in my visions. I starting praying about it. *Father GOD, where am I to go? Please lead me into your direction.*

My two logical choices to find work and a place to stay on probation were Oklahoma City or Tulsa. As I prayed, the Holy Spirit made clear that Tulsa was GOD's plan for me. Shortly after, Mom wrote to let me know she'd found me a room at a sober living facility in Tulsa. It wasn't months but just a short time after getting my license when I returned from my hospital job to find my supervising officer waiting for me.

"Cruz, pack your bags," he told me solemnly. "You're out of here in the morning."

I froze, a sharp jolt stabbing into my heart. My first thought was that something had gone horribly wrong and I was being shipped back to Crabtree or some similar facility. Then the officer broke into a wide grin. "Hey, don't you get it? Your release papers came through. You're going home. As of tomorrow, you're a free man!"

Right then, I just lost it, bursting into tears of joy. Returning to my bunk to pack, I began praising and thanking GOD. Not just for my release, but for this entire incredible journey. For the blessing that getting arrested and sent to prison had turned out to be. I knew now that it was because my heavenly Father loved me that he'd let me hit rock-bottom so I could become the person he'd called me to be. And because he loved me, he'd never left me alone. He'd sent me so many kind strangers along the way.

Strangers who'd become friends and mentors. He'd been there for me interceding to keep me safe. He'd helped me to not lose faith.

Thank you, GOD! Thank you, heavenly Father!

On March 24, 2010, two years and eight months after I'd walked into that courtroom in Oklahoma City to turn myself in, I was released from Frederick Community Work Center. I would have to wear an ankle monitor for the foreseeable future. I would have to abide by a curfew and be supervised by a probation officer. But I was free.

These last three years had given me a whole new appreciation for the basics of life I'd once taken for granted. Waking up on my own time. Taking a shower when I want. Eating the food I choose when I want to eat it. Getting to choose where I want to go and what I want to do. I remain so grateful to GOD for these every single day. Not everyone around the world has those blessings, whether because they are in prison or living in great poverty or in a country that doesn't have such freedoms.

Now the new Abe Cruz just had to convince those who'd known the old Abe Cruz that I'd changed. I was free, but I was also a convicted felon. I had faith in the visions GOD had given me in prison. But for those to come true, I would have to demonstrate to everyone else that I could turn the statistical negative stereotype of an ex-con into a major success story.

CHAPTER TWENTY-FIVE
ABE 2.0

THEY SAY PRISON CHANGES YOUR LIFE for better or worse. Statistically, it's usually for the worse. All odds are against a convicted felon, and too often no one is willing to help them or give them a second chance at life. That's a reality you have to accept as an ex-con, taking responsibility for your past actions and the consequences of them.

When Mom had encouraged me to ask GOD for a second chance in life, I'd promised GOD to do everything in my power to represent him—and I'd meant it! You have to mean it if you want GOD to take your promises seriously. I'd gone into prison broken-down, wounded, lost. Over the past almost three years, GOD had been training me and building me up to be smarter, stronger, and a faithful soldier for him. My deep prayer times had shown me a clear path and mission for turning this negative of being an ex-con into a positive. I'd endured pain and suffering for doing wrong in the past. Now I was prepared to accept more pain and suffering but this time for doing GOD's great work.

I'm thankful I'd prepared myself because being free didn't turn out as wonderful as I'd dreamed. A corrections officer drove me to Tulsa, where my first stop was meeting with my probation officer and being fitted with an ankle monitor. My PO explained that I had just fourteen days to get a job. Along with rent and other expenses, I'd have to pay $75 a month for my ankle monitor, so there was major pressure to start earning.

Then I was introduced to my new lodgings. The sober living house had three bedrooms, one bathroom, a small shared kitchen—and six residents. The others were all there for drug and alcohol abuse, so random searches and regular urine testing were part of the house rules. I quickly saw that some of them were still using.

This scared me stiff since if a search turned up drugs, it would just be my word that I had no part in it. The last thing I wanted was to end up back in prison because I was rooming with a meth-head. Unlike prison, there were no guards or so much as a supervisor living onsite. I didn't even have a private room I could lock myself into, and in fact, I was more scared sleeping there than I ever was in prison.

As soon as I'd been walked through the house rules, evening curfew, and other details, I headed out to the nearest public transport to start my job search. I had a simple plan. I'd walk into a gym and start working out. Once they saw my fitness and that I knew what I was doing, I'd mention that I was looking for employment.

My plan worked perfectly, and I was soon sitting down with the manager to discuss a job. But the moment I mentioned my ankle monitor, their interest evaporated. I was disappointed and a bit hurt, but I could understand their hesitation. After all, they had no idea who I was and what situation had led to the ankle monitor, just that I was an ex-con. This was only the first day, and there were other gyms.

I visited several other gyms and real estate offices as well, since I had ample experience there and could get good references from my boss in LA. But each time interest evaporated as soon as they found out I'd been in prison. I finally took a bus back to the sober living home, since if my ankle monitor didn't show me back by seven p.m., I'd be hearing from my probation officer.

For the next ten days, I hit the streets by seven a.m., returning home just in time for curfew. Each day I'd target a different neighborhood, visiting every gym, fitness center, and real estate office. But each day I received the same response.

On the eleventh day, I received a call from my probation officer. "Cruz, why am I not hearing you've got a job yet?"

"I've applied all over the city," I explained. "But no one will hire me."

When I gave him a list of places where I'd applied, he blew up. "These are all gyms and real estate offices. Why haven't you applied at McDonalds? Burger King? Starbucks?"

"I didn't even think of it," I answered. "I mean, I'm pretty overqualified for those."

I wasn't trying to be arrogant. Considering the kind of jobs and earnings I'd had before prison, it hadn't even occurred to me to look at no-skill minimum-wage entry-level jobs. But now my probation officer really blew up.

"You think ex-cons can be picky about what they get? That you're too good for fast food? You get back out there because you've got just seventy-two hours left. If you don't have a job by then, I'm sending you back to prison."

I was pretty freaked out by the time I got off the phone. I'd been locked up for almost three years, and now after just eleven days of freedom, I was in danger of being sent back inside. Calling my mom, I poured out my situation. As always, she reassured me. "*M'ijo, cálmate* [my son, calm yourself]. GOD is with you. Let's pray together and ask GOD for direction to finding the right job."

By the end of our prayer time together, I was a little calmer but still stressed. I had one more job possibility, but it was a long shot. I'd gone into a gym not far from the sober living house, All American Fitness, a regional chain with numerous gyms in Tulsa, Oklahoma City, and other locations. They'd offered me an interview but for a different gym on the far side of the Tulsa metropolitan area. The interview was for nine a.m., and by bus it would take a good three hours to get there. Since every other gym had turned me down, it hardly seemed worth the time investment—most of a day there and back—just to be told no again.

Unless I could somehow get a ride out there, which would at least leave me most of the day to job-search elsewhere. Unfortunately, I didn't have a single friend or even acquaintance with wheels in Tulsa except my probation officer, who certainly wasn't going to offer.

That's when I remembered what John Helstrom had told me when I'd been at Creek County jail. "God is in the business of working miracles . . . God has something special for you, Abe . . . Anything you need, just look me up."

That had been almost two years ago. Had he been serious about his offer? With all the inmates he'd dealt with, would he even remember me? The only way to find out was to take a leap of faith and call.

To my relief, John sounded delighted to hear from me and instantly volunteered to drive me when I explained about my interview. Cheerfully, he added, "Just one condition, though. I'll take you to your interview. In return, you go to church with me this Sunday."

I was more than happy to agree. The next morning John picked me up at the sober living home. I'd dressed for success in a light-blue button-down shirt and black slacks. We arrived at the interview location with time to spare. Before I could get out of the car, John asked, "Do you mind if I pray with you before you go in."

"Yes please, I would be so grateful," I responded.

We both bowed our heads while John prayed a powerful prayer asking God's favor and blessing on this job opportunity. I felt so deeply touched by his loving kindness. Thanking him, I walked into the gym where I introduced myself humbly but confidently to the All American Fitness vice president of operations Scott Matlock. He seemed impressed with my résumé until he noticed the employment gap between 2007 and 2010.

"What have you been up to since 2007?" he asked.

Our easy conversation turned suddenly very awkward. I had to be honest with him, so I explained how I'd made some wrong choices and had just been released from prison eleven days ago. "But I've changed my life around, and I'm looking to make a new start. I'm eager to start working immediately and work hard. In fact, all I can do right now is work and go home, so I'd happy to work as many hours as you need."

He looked at me for a moment, then nodded. "Okay, Abe, I'll give you a chance."

Just like that I had a job. Praising GOD for his blessing, I immediately found a quiet spot to call John Helstrom. Excitedly, I told him, "Your prayer worked! I got the job!"

> "GOD uses people as his instruments to impact other lives." —Abe Cruz

"Amen, congratulations," he answered. "Now get ready for church Sunday morning. I'll see you then."

After the interview, Scott allowed me to stay and get familiar with the gym since I'd be there every day. Changing to work-out clothes, I had a great training session, then walked next door to a nutrition supplement shop for a post-workout protein shake. While the owner was making my shake, a customer walked in. I was wearing a tight, sleeveless compression shirt and must have looked the part of a fitness trainer because the customer asked me what kind of supplements I'd recommend. The store owner gave me a nod, so I walked the customer through a selection.

The owner, a kind older lady, was so pleased with the sale she insisted on giving me my shake for free, then asked if I'd be interested in a job. I agreed to work for her any hours I wasn't scheduled at the gym. Talk about the power of prayer! Just a day earlier, I'd been threatened with going back to prison because I couldn't get a job. Now I had two.

I called my probation officer to share my exciting news. He didn't believe me until I put him in contact with my two new bosses. At least he no longer had a pretext to send me back to prison.

That Sunday morning, John Helstrom along with his wife Kate picked me up, and I walked with them into a church for the first time since going to prison. The church was huge with thousands in attendance from many different ethnicities. The preaching, singing, loving atmosphere, and warm welcome from John and Kate's friends had such an emotional impact on me. All the pain, grief, shame, and suffering of these past years rose inside of me along with so much joy and light and hope for the future.

At the end, the pastor asked for anyone ready to give their life to Christ to come to the front of the sanctuary. All around me people were walking down the aisles. The Helstroms didn't say anything to me or suggest I go forward. But I found myself on my feet and walking down to the front. I felt such an overwhelming sense of God's love that I just fell to my hands and knees, crying uncontrollably, waves of happiness and thanksgiving sweeping over me.

Suddenly I felt a touch on my shoulder. A Latino man about my age lifted me to my feet. He didn't even ask me any questions, but just put his arms around me and hugged me while we cried together. He kept saying, "Brother, it's going to be okay. God loves you. I love you. It's going to be okay."

When I calmed down a bit, he said, "Brother, I'm going to pray for you."

After he prayed, he introduced himself as José Miranda, one of the church pastors. From that day forward, José became one more of a long line of amazing people God put into my life to bless me. He has been a spiritual mentor, brother, and overall great friend to me. Seven years later, I was one of his groomsmen at his wedding.

As I've gotten to know incredible human beings like Oscar, Ken, John, José, I've come to see that God uses people as his instruments to impact other lives. Sometimes this may just be for a single encounter or for a particular season of life. Sometimes if we're blessed and fortunate, it may be for a lifetime.

CHAPTER TWENTY-SIX
NEW BLESSINGS, NEW CHALLENGES

My new work schedule meant being up by four a.m. to catch two separate bus lines in order to reach my first job at the supplement store by nine a.m. I worked there until two p.m., then headed to the gym to work out before starting my training sessions with clients. These often lasted well into the evening, so there was no way to be back at the sober living facility by our seven p.m. curfew. Once he'd confirmed I was actually working, my probation officer gave me permission for the longer hours.

It was a hectic schedule but sure better than being locked up. After a couple weeks, my kind boss at the supplement shop decided it was ridiculous for me to be wasting three hours each way, so she started picking me up and dropping me off. Not long after that, I was promoted to a manager position at the gym. This increased my income enough to buy a 1989 beat-up red Acura Integra for just $900. Having my own transport again was such an amazing feeling of freedom.

Now I didn't have to wake up so early. But I'd already decided—monitor or no monitor—that I was going to compete in a local bodybuilding competition coming up that summer. So I still got up at five a.m. to train at the gym before work. Thankfully, since my release I'd been able to get treatment for the acne scarring, so mirrors no longer scared me away.

By now my life had fallen into a stable pattern—my two jobs, working out, and attending church with the Helstroms on Sundays. In my free time, I educated myself about the Internet. This had come a long ways in the three years since I'd had access to a computer. I was fascinated by search engines like Google or Yahoo, which allowed me to type in any question and get an answer.

I still had absolute faith in the vision GOD had given me for my future, and I carried a folder with all the sketches and scribbled ideas of my "business plan from prison" everywhere I went. I researched how to register my Forever Faith brand, copyright my comic book and movie script, start a clothing line. I also researched changes in style. Baggy jeans had given way to skinny or wide-bottom. Longer camisole tops were replacing crop tops. Neon colors were in.

In all this, I was finding it tough to let people get close to me here in Tulsa. When people start getting close to you, they want to know all about you. It was easy to explain that my accent and mannerisms were different because I came from LA. Explaining why I was in Tulsa was more difficult. When I did open up to a few clients, they acted as though a convicted felon was some kind of contagious disease and immediately demanded to be switched to a new trainer.

One incident was especially painful. Some money had come up short, less than a hundred dollars, but I was immediately accused of stealing it. I was deeply hurt because I'd thought I had a good relationship with this person. But I was also worried since even a false accusation could bring all my hard work tumbling down and send me back to prison for a parole violation.

"I don't steal!" I insisted. "I didn't go to prison because I was a thief!"

Just then, another person stepped forward and pointed out the missing money, which had been laid to one side. My accuser apologized profusely, and I accepted the apology. But though our working relationship continued, it was never the same. It hit me painfully that no matter how hard I worked or what I said and did, for the rest of my life I'd be labeled a convicted felon. That was my new reality.

But I also realized that since this was my reality, I needed to accept it, even embrace it, and figure out how to use it as a positive stepping-stone instead of trying to hide from it. A true leader doesn't waste their time on the problem but focuses on the solution. No matter our challenges and obstacles in life, we must figure out how to overcome them and succeed.

In my case, I chose to stop being embarrassed by my past or ankle monitor but to use those to share my message of Forever Faith. That was what GOD had called me to do, and if I was to be his representative in this world, I needed to get past being focused on my own negative self-image.

This was especially crucial since that very weekend was the bodybuilding competition I'd been preparing for over the past three months since my release. I didn't expect to win or even place. And I had no idea what kind of response I'd get standing up there in nothing but briefs and an ankle monitor. But I was determined not to let accusations and judgmental attitudes derail me from fulfilling this first big step toward the vision and mission GOD had given me in prison.

The day of the competition, I walked out onto the stage with a confident stride and big smile. The event was packed out with almost a thousand in attendance. I could see people pointing to my ankle monitor and laughing at me. But I refused to let that get me down. I ended up coming in eighth, and altogether it was a great experience.

From that point, GOD opened the door to blessing after blessing. For every hater, I met far more kind people willing to give me a second chance. One client managed several apartment complexes and helped me get a small apartment of my own. Saying goodbye to the sober living facility was another big blessing.

But this still wasn't the vision GOD had given me for my future. Listening to others around me, I quickly saw that prison inmates weren't the only ones losing their faith. Sometimes because of tragedy or a major life crisis. Other times for seemingly trivial reasons like GOD not giving them a job they'd prayed for or even a new car.

One thing I'd learned the hard way these last few years was that you can't just ask GOD to take away all your problems or give you everything you want. You need to first ask GOD what *his* plans are to make you the best you can be. You also need the self-motivation to get out there and do your part in coming up with a solution. Above all, you need to keep the faith. Everything else we get all panicked and frustrated about will come and go. Faith is forever.

But how to get this message out to all the hurting, anxious people I'd never meet in person who were in need of encouragement? I'd continued taking my "business plan from prison" folder to the gym and had shared it with a number of clients and gym employees. Most laughed or figured it just wasn't realistic for an ex-con. But one guy immediately saw the possibilities.

"These are really cool!" he told me, looking over my designs. "Really inspirational. You know, my aunt owns a shop that does custom printing for clothing. I think she'd be interested in these."

> "It isn't enough to just sit back and say you have faith. If you have true faith, you'll get up and go after those goals." —Abe Cruz

That was the beginning of the Forever Faith clothing brand. The aunt was so impressed she actually fronted $500 worth of printed clothing with my designs. We sold these at the gym and made enough profit to pay her and print some more.

Seeing the potential, I got on the phone with my brother David, who was still living in LA. Like most siblings, we hadn't always gotten along, especially in our teens. But when I really needed him, he'd always been there, especially after my arrest. I told him all about what had happened to me in prison, my forty-day fast, and the vision GOD had given me for my future.

"You've got to come here to Tulsa," I urged. "Forever Faith is going to be something big that will motivate and inspire people and change their lives. I want you to be part of it. I want to do this together as brothers."

David not only agreed to come, but invested some of his own money into the project. We shared an apartment, and he also worked with me at the gym, which gave us a steady income. We printed our first set of T-shirts and were soon selling them out of the trunk of my car as well as at the gym. Through a jeweler I met at the gym, we created the same Forever Faith dog tags I'd featured in my comic book.

Every product carried our logo Forever Faith. We also created inspirational slogans. GOD First, Me Second. Just Believe. Mindset of Champions. If You Don't Believe in Yourself No One Else Will. We set up a Facebook page and a website. Soon David and I were working day and night to fill orders. We'd bring each new print-run home to our apartment, package the order, then run down to Staples to ship the packages.

I'd learned from my business experience in college that if you demand attention you'll get it. Nor had I forgotten those flashy sports cars my "upline" leader had driven around campus to promote their brand. As soon as we had enough profits, David was able to buy a gorgeous silver Mercedes Benz CLK430. We wrapped both sides, including doors and windows, with the Forever Faith logo.

Now we were a driving billboard with a powerful positive message. We began receiving bulk orders. Within a month's time, we were selling in seven different stores throughout Oklahoma while orders came from all over the country. We plowed the profits back into our flourishing business. It helped that I was no longer wasting everything I earned on clubbing and girls!

Then one day in early December 2010, a man walked into the gym who would become the next incredible mentor and blessing GOD sent into my life. He was older, white-haired, about my height, and extremely fit for his age. Approaching the front desk, he asked, "Whose is that Mercedes out there with the Forever Faith logo?"

The receptionist pointed him in my direction. Walking over, he introduced himself. "Hi. I'm Fred Bassett."

Shaking his hand, I asked, "So how can I help you?"

As gym manager, I assumed this was a customer service query. Instead, he responded, "I saw your beautiful car out there and checked out your website. A great inspirational message!"

Our website was pretty simple, so I knew he had to be referring to my favorite Jim Rohn quote I'd placed front and center: "The greatest service to mankind is finding a way to serve many people."

"You've got a great brand," Fred went on. "I love the philosophy and message of Forever Faith. But I didn't see any actual clothing catalog on the site or means to make an online purchase. I'd like to offer my services as a photographer free of charge."

Wow! My first impression of Fred was of a very kind, loving, caring person. Not to mention a lot of energy. That impression hasn't changed as that's exactly who he is along with being a very godly, devout man of faith. But at the time I'll admit I was leery of his offer. I mean, this guy didn't know me at all. Why would he be so generous to a total stranger? And what would he think when he found out who I really was—an ex-con wearing an ankle monitor?

On the other hand, we'd been looking for a photographer to upgrade our website. To this point, our nationwide sales had come through fairly low-resolution photos of our clothing posted on Facebook. I knew that wasn't good enough if we were to grow the Forever Faith brand.

I think Fred saw my unease because he quickly added, "Look, you don't need to make any decisions now. The offer stands if you're interested. And I'd like to take you out to lunch sometime, so you can tell me about this brand and how you came up with it."

I didn't accept his lunch invitation immediately, but he came back to the gym almost every day. As he worked out, I saw him observing my interactions with clients and how I was running the gym. I know now he wanted to evaluate if I had the people and business skills to make a success out of the Forever Faith brand.

I finally met Fred for lunch at Rib Crib, a barbecue restaurant right next to the gym. He proved very easy to talk to and so kind and compassionate I found myself pouring out my entire story from my father leaving to how my entire journey to rock-bottom and back was a blessing from GOD that had led to Forever Faith.

When I finished, he didn't pass judgment as I'd expected. He just shook his head in astonishment. "Abe, you're an amazing young man. I believe in you and your mission from GOD. And I'd like to help you with it any way I can."

Fred went on to share his own backstory. His profession was IT (information technology), and he'd held leadership positions with American Airlines, EDS (Electronic Data Systems), and Saber Holdings for over three decades. He'd also started a couple small businesses. One of his hobbies was photography so he owned all the cameras and other equipment to do professional photo shoots. Another was judging at dog shows for the American Kennel Club (AKC), as well as a celebrity judge for dog shows across Asia, Latin America, Europe, Australia, and Canada.

But that still left him plenty of free time now that he was retired. He began asking questions. "So have you set up your LLC (Limited Liability Company)? Have you registered and trademarked your brand? Do you have your tax ID number so you can work with wholesalers?"

Of course I'd done none of those things. Other than printing clothing and offering it for sale, I knew nothing about setting up a business.

"See, that's something I can help you with," Fred went on. "I truly believe GOD brought me here to meet you and has given me a spiritual connection with you. I have the experience you need in IT and the business world. I don't want to spend my retirement years sitting around playing Sudoku. I want to do something that will make a difference, and I'd be really excited to get involved in your mission from GOD. I'm not a wealthy man, but I could consider helping financially too as things get going. So think over my offer, and let's talk again soon."

It all sounded good, but this was moving way too fast. Respectfully but firmly, I told him, "I really appreciate your offer. But I need to pray for GOD's direction on this and talk it over with my brother."

"I understand completely and am in total agreement," Fred answered. "If you change your mind, just give me a call. Meanwhile, I'll be praying too."

I told David about the offer, and we prayed together for direction. The more I prayed, the more I could see that Fred was exactly what we needed to take Forever Faith to the next level. He had the business experience, IT and computer skills, and legal knowledge we were lacking. And we couldn't keep growing without some serious financial investment.

Bottom line, we'd been asking GOD to supply those needs, and GOD had answered our prayers. Fred Bassett *was* GOD's answer.

Picking up the phone, I called Fred and told him we'd count ourselves blessed to have him come on board. I've never had reason to regret that decision.

Throughout my journey, I've been privileged to have so many great men guiding and directing me. But I believe GOD brought Fred into my life at this particular season for all the right reasons at just the right time. For the first time since my biological father left me, I actually came to feel that I had a father in my life again, and I call him Pops to this day.

CHAPTER TWENTY-SEVEN
BIRTH OF A MOVEMENT

POPS' PARTNERSHIP PUT FOREVER FAITH on fast track. He produced our first wholesale catalog, which we could then email to prospective clients. Our first cross-border purchase came from Mexico City, which officially made us an international brand. We started getting requests for team uniforms and orders too big to print locally, so David moved back to LA to set up production there.

But just selling clothing, however inspirational, was also not the vision GOD had given me. That vision included sharing GOD's message and serving others directly. Working in the gym put me into contact with people from all walks of life around Tulsa. Just about the time I met Pops, one of those contacts resulted in an invitation to speak to the Oklahoma state legislature on behalf of rehabilitation for convicted felons. Addressing the legislature on December 3, 2010, was my first serious public speaking engagement. More than that, I felt deeply honored to be a mouthpiece for many other felons who needed help but didn't have this kind of opportunity to communicate their circumstances.

Just a couple months later, a Tulsa city leader came across the Forever Faith brand in one of the boutiques that carried it. She was so intrigued by the message that she contacted me to learn more about it. That led to a photo shoot and front-page story in the Tulsa World newspaper. The headline read: "Man Finds Inspiration While Serving Time In Prison." The article included a photo of me working out with the Forever Faith logo across my chest.

A hundred thousand copies were printed along with the article being posted online. Everywhere I went now, people knew who I was. That led to many more speaking engagements.

One of these was at a boys home for troubled youth. These teens had every reason to be losing faith. Most were runaways, had one or both parents in prison, or had never known their biological parents. They needed most of all to know someone cared about them. So while I focused on helping them understand the urgency of making right choices, I also shared what I'd learned at rock-bottom—that they have a heavenly Father who will always love them and never leave them.

As a brand, we also participated in raising funds for leukemia, sponsored a local youth dance team, and other community outreaches. All this was taking a lot of time from my job at the gym. By now David was back in LA meeting with manufacturers and developing partnerships to expand our clothing line in LA's fashion district. Pops remained the rock of our growing enterprise. One day he suggested I move in with him and his wife Janet so I could quit my job and not have to worry about rent while we built up Forever Faith.

Janet is an incredibly kind, loving person. Allowing an ex-con she barely knew to move into their home had to be one of the craziest ideas she'd heard. But she said she'd pray about it, and she did. That Sunday at her church, the scripture readings and message were all about trust and forgiveness. She came home and told Pops God had given her his answer. From the day I moved in, both of them treated me as a son. They will always be second parents to me.

By now David was really growing our sports apparel division in LA. We'd expanded to track suits, sweatshirts, team uniforms, all kinds of fitness apparel, as well as sports bags. One day I received a phone call from a television producer in Hollywood.

"Hey, Abe, we've heard how you were released from prison and have been able to turn your nightmare situation into a dream come true. We'd really like you to consider coming on our show, Millionaire Matchmaker, to tell your story. We're especially interested in two brothers bringing a positive message of Christian faith to the world."

Another wow! Millionaire Matchmaker was a reality show hosted by real-life matchmaker Patti Stenger that helped millionaire bachelors and bachelorettes find the mate of their dreams. I wasn't looking for a relationship—in part, because I was already pretty sure I'd met the girl of my dreams, as you'll see later. But the show would give me another opportunity to share the message of Forever Faith. This time to millions of viewers. David had his own story to tell, so doing the show together as brothers was an even bigger blessing.

I called David to give him the good news. But I'd forgotten one crucial detail. I was still on my ankle monitor and prohibited from leaving Oklahoma. Sure enough, when I talked to my probation officer about traveling to LA to film the episode, he gave me a flat no. As with my first job, he also made it clear he thought I was lying to flee my probation.

This time I knew I needed to make a stand. A major point of probation is rehabilitation so the ex-prisoner can become a useful, successful member of society. Millionaire Matchmaker was a big potential boost to my business and future, so my probation officer had no legitimate right to keep me from it. More than that, this offer was right out of the vision I'd been given in prison, and I knew it came from GOD. So I refused to back down.

It took a lawyer, several months, and proof from the producer that this was a legitimate engagement. But in early summer, Pops and I drove to the probation officer one last time to take my final mug-shot and have my ankle monitor removed. I was now free to travel the world so long as I stayed away from trouble. *Thank you, Father GOD!*

The best part of being free to travel was seeing Mom again. While we talked by phone all the time, I hadn't seen her in person since she'd stood by me to turn myself in, so it was a very emotional reunion.

Reconnecting with Oscar Cepeida and his family was equally emotional. While I knew how disappointed Oscar had been at my wrong life choices, I also knew he'd never stopped praying for me and believing in me. Like the loving father in the parable Jesus told about the Prodigal Son (Luke 15:11-32), he welcomed me back with open arms, forgave me for letting him down, and remains one of my closest friends and strongest supporters.

Now instead of David living with me in Tulsa, I was living with him in LA while we did the taping for Millionaire Matchmaker. Though that was far from all we were doing. Since neither David nor I had experience in launching a clothing brand, Pops continued to be our mentor and go-to guy for any issues, problems, and questions. With his advice, we struck a partnership with a major international clothing manufacturer based in LA.

> "If in your heart, mind, soul, and spirit you are doing everything in the best manner you can possibly do, then you are a champion."
>
> —Abe Cruz

Being back in LA meant I could also pursue contacts with pro-athletes, coaches, schools, filmmakers, and agents I'd done modeling and acting shoots for in the past. We soon had a list of pro athletes sporting Forever Faith apparel, including NFL stars like Shareece Wright, Allen Bradford, Eric Dickerson, Anthony Miller, Christian Okoye, Vince Ferragamo, and Olympic gold medalist Ron Brown.

I was also speaking at high school assemblies. I filmed a documentary called Fashion and Culture in LA, which included outreach to the homeless sponsored by Forever Faith. We were now sponsoring a dozen youth sports programs from football to basketball, paying forward all those sponsorships that had jumpstarted my own athletic career as a kid. Among the many school teams now wearing Forever Faith uniforms was my alma mater St. Paul. We sponsored a kids art day. I guest-interviewed on radio shows and even at the MTV Music Awards.

The Millionaire Matchmaker episode finally aired October 2011. Though neither of us found our soulmates, it was a great experience for David and me. I received a lot of practical advice on courtship from Patti Stenger, which I really appreciated since I'd been out of the dating game for almost five years. The episode ended up being one of the highest-rated of the show's seven seasons and is still frequently aired in re-runs.

And just as I'd anticipated when I'd battled with my probation officer to pursue this opportunity, the show blew wide-open the doors to fulfill every other aspect of the vision GOD had given me in prison. David and I were both bombarded with fan mail and other opportunities. We quickly learned that not all opportunities were good ones. Pops with his wisdom, experience, and ability to assess people became our screener.

One day Pops spotted a request for a photoshoot from a world-famous fitness photographer, Noel Daganta. He'd done covers and feature articles for the biggest magazines in the fitness world. Noel was interested in a cover shoot of me in bodybuilder poses as well as some feature articles on my fitness routines, including my water bag workout and others I'd developed in prison. Thanks to Noel, I soon found myself on the cover and in feature articles for *Iron Man, Muscle and Fitness USA, Physique, Firm and Fitness Canada, GNC Muscle & Body, Men's Fitness, Men's Health,* and other magazines. Once again GOD was fulfilling the vision he'd shown me in prison.

Then a friend introduced me to former NFL star Ron Brown, known as the NFL's fastest man alive since he'd won a gold medal in track at the 1984 Olympics. For all his fame, Ron is a very humble, quiet, caring person. Having grown up in a poor LA neighborhood himself, he understood overcoming obstacles and was excited about the Forever Faith message.

Ron Brown in turn introduced me to his good friend NFL Hall of Famer Eric Dickerson. A committed Christian, Eric had established the Eric Dickerson Foundation, which focused on providing positive influences to at-risk youth through sports, education, and leadership. Each year his foundation funded a number of youth sports camps around the country, including at Camp Pendleton in San Diego.

Through Ron and Eric, Forever Faith was able to partner with the foundation to create T-shirts and backpacks for the camp. It was a dream come true to see these young athletes and the various NFL players volunteering at the camp all wearing Forever Faith apparel. Volunteer organizations like these had made such an impact on my childhood, and it was a great joy to come full circle in helping a new generation of young athletes pursue their dreams.

A few days after the camp, we received an invitation to outfit Evander Holyfield, eight-time world champion boxer, with Forever Faith apparel for an upcoming photo shoot. Like Eric Dickerson, Evander was a devout Christian and a very humble, kind person. I felt so blessed to spend time with him and hear his story as well as share the story behind Forever Faith. We ended up outfitting a second photo shoot for Evander's children as well.

Then out of nowhere, I received a phone call from Ron Brown. "Hey, Abe, I'm heading to your office, but I'm running late. I've got a friend coming, Deebo, who should be there any minute."

I couldn't believe what I was hearing. "Deebo? You mean, like the actor from *Friday* and *Fifth Element* Deebo? Like the pro wrestler Zeus from the WWF Deebo?"

"Yeah, that's right. But call him Tiny. He's a good friend of mine. I told him all about Forever Faith, and he wants to meet you. He's a big believer and has a powerful testimony of his own life journey to GOD. Just keep him entertained until I get there."

Tom "Tiny" Lister had been a big name in pro wrestling in the 1990s, which led to a successful acting career. Born blind in his right eye, he'd once thought the birth defect was a curse from GOD until GOD showed him what a blessing it was in keeping him out of gang life and shaping his acting career. Tiny Lister has a powerful ministry to urban youth and speaks on Christian TV channels, radios, churches, and other faith-based events.

Since I was a big fan, I was pretty nervous about introducing myself. I headed outside just as an all-black Range Rover with twenty-two-inch rims pulled into the parking lot. The man climbing out was the opposite of his nickname—about 6'5" and three hundred pounds. We hit it off instantly. I shared the Forever Faith story and how prison had been my own biggest life blessing. He'd grown up in Compton, a south LA community with the highest crime rate in California, notorious for gang violence between the Bloods and Crips, so he understood my journey.

Spotting my cover of *Iron Man Magazine* lying on my desk, Tiny picked it up. "This is you?"

"Yes, sir," I responded. I went on to tell him how one of the visions I'd had in prison, along with speaking, magazines, and clothing design, was acting.

"I got you!" he said immediately. "I'll put you in some movies."

He kept his word. Tiny once shared with me a quote from the Bible about GOD restoring the years we've lost when we repent and turn back to him (Joel 2:25). I believe it absolutely because I've seen GOD working in my life to redeem and restore all those years I'd thrown away from the very first day of my sentencing when that guard had assured me in Spanish, "*Todo va estar bien* [everything will be fine]. *Dios está contigo* [GOD is with you]."

My "business plan from prison" was becoming a reality so quickly it felt I was living life with the fast forward button on full velocity. Maybe it seemed that way because prison life had been very much on slow motion. I had mental flashbacks to those lost years of Playboy Mansion parties, clubbing, Las Vegas. Here we were five years later and less than two years since being released from prison, and all the visions GOD had given me were coming true.

But I hadn't forgotten either my vow to GOD that if he gave me a second chance I would live to put him first. Every time a new element of my vision came true, I prayed that GOD would keep me on track. I knew I couldn't continue my mission or receive GOD's blessing if I allowed myself to get caught up again with women, partying, making money, and all the other distractions I'd let take control so many times in the past.

With all the frenzy and attention, I asked Pops to keep me in check and let me know if I was drifting off mission. I was so deeply thankful and still am for having Pops in my life. He hasn't just been my business partner but friend, advisor, and guardian angel sent by God to guide and mentor me.

Then one day I received a phone call that redirected my life journey in a whole new direction and would change me forever.

CHAPTER TWENTY-EIGHT
LOVE OF MY LIFE

IT WAS SHORTLY AFTER I MET POPS WHEN the most incredible woman I'd ever known walked into my workplace—and my life. Of Central Asian heritage, she was slim, beautiful, petite, with long, silky black hair, big, dark eyes, and a smile that takes your breath away.

Though already fit, she was wanting to improve her general health so she'd purchased a personal training package. As we began training together, she was quiet and reserved, always professional in demeanor with no flirting. And believe me with a smile like that, I tried!

On my end, I'd rarely felt so insecure. In my early twenties before prison, I'd seen myself as a player, always with several good-looking women on my arm, throwing money around to impress them. My only attempt at a serious relationship had ended with a broken heart. And of course I hadn't been around women at all for several years. So despite everything GOD had taught me in prison, this was one area where I was still pretty immature. I could see she was way out of my league, but I sure wanted to get to know her.

Slowly over the weeks as I worked with her, she began opening up. I told her about my family and where I was born and raised. She told me about immigrating to the United States in her late teens and how she and some family members had developed a successful local business. That she'd taught herself such fluent, grammatical English showed me she was highly intelligent and with a work ethic that matched her beauty.

Then one day in the middle of training, she asked me if I'd like to go out after our session. I immediately froze. Of course I'd like to go out with her! What guy on the planet wouldn't? But I hadn't told her yet about my ankle monitor or that I had to rush home after work because I was on a curfew. Turning bright-red, I stammered out that I was too busy at the moment but maybe on some future date.

I could see my excuses had hurt her. When I didn't hear from her to set up the next training session, I was worried my awkward behavior had lost her for good. Then one day out of the blue, I received a text from her. It read, "I think I like my trainer."

Dumbfounded, I stared at the text. Had this been meant for me, or had she thumb-texted the wrong person. I finally texted back, keeping my response light, "LOL. Is this for me?"

She immediately texted back, "LOL. I'm so sorry. I meant to send that to a friend."

Intentional or not, her words put me over the moon with joy. I texted back, "No big deal. So when are you coming in again to train?"

We set a time to train the very next evening. When she came, I shared honestly about the ankle monitor, my prison journey, and my curfew. She didn't judge me at all but just accepted me as the person she'd gotten to know these last weeks. I then asked if I could take her out the following Friday when my schedule could fit in a date before curfew. I was thrilled when she agreed.

Friday morning was like waking up to a championship game day. Hyped with anticipation, I texted her, "Have a great day. Excited to see you later for dinner."

She responded with a smiley-face. I had finished work and was getting ready for our date when I received another text. My emotions immediately plummeted. *I knew it was all too good to believe! She's cancelling on me.*

But the actual text was even less welcome than a cancellation: "I can't find a babysitter for my son. I might have to reschedule."

My heart stopped in mid-beat, then dropped into my shoes. Her son? She'd never mentioned a son. How old was he? Where was his father?

Chaotic emotions and childhood memories flooded through me. My father screaming, yelling, smashing a mirror while Mom cried and I cowered under the couch. My father disappearing when I was four, never to contact me again. I knew nothing about being a father because I'd never had a father. All I'd wanted here was to go out for an enjoyable date with a gorgeous woman. At twenty-nine, the last thing on my radar was assuming any kind of responsibility for someone else's kid!

Then it hit me how selfish I sounded. After all, my mom had been a single mother in a similar position. And if my father had walked out on us, GOD had sent many great father figures to be a blessing in my life. I'd seen how Oscar and others treated their kids. How they treated me even though I wasn't their biological son. I'd asked GOD to give *me* a second chance. What kind of man was I if I wasn't willing to give a single mom and her son a chance?

I texted back, "No worries. Bring your son. I would love to meet him."

> "When you put GOD first, you'll automatically become the best version of yourself that you can be." —Abe Cruz

That was the first step to my really growing up emotionally. I met this wonderful woman and her son at Outback Steak House. He was just turning eight years old and clearly the bright star in her world just as David and I had been for my mom. Like his mom, he was quiet and reserved at first, extremely intelligent, and well-mannered.

Over dinner, all three of us began opening up to each other. This young man's father had left them just about the same age I'd been when my father walked out. When I shared how I'd grown up without a father, I had his immediate attention.

I explained to him how his mom was like my mom—a Super Mom taking care of him all by herself. Then I found myself giving him the same assurance Oscar had once given me. "Don't you worry. Your mom loves you with all her heart, and everything's going to be fine. Just make sure you always love, respect, and protect your mom."

From that point on, this was no longer about Abe Cruz getting to hang out with a gorgeous woman. It was about becoming part of the journey of two very special people. This was a package deal, and if I wanted to be in her life, I would also be in her son's. It took me back again to my own father. To this kid's father.

How can a man leave something he created behind? I asked myself, *How can a man walk away from his own flesh and blood?*

Especially a great kid like this one. I was pretty sure I'd found a once-in-a-lifetime, love-of-my-life woman. But I was also still on that fast-forward, trying to stay focused on getting the Forever Faith brand off the ground, fulfilling my "business plan from prison," speaking, and media engagements. Which included moving back to LA and filming the Millionaire Matchmaker episode.

I'd told Honey, as I'd begun calling her and still do, that I might be relocated to LA at any time. She understood and completely supported me following my dreams. Just a short time after our date, I got the green light to remove my ankle monitor and travel to LA. At first we both thought this would be short-term, just long enough to tape the show and get the new manufacturing partnership off the ground. But then Forever Faith's success began to snowball.

I finally had to admit, "I don't know when I'll be back. But it's going to be awhile."

Not long after, Honey called me. "Look, I miss you. I want to spend time with you, whatever it takes. If I buy my own ticket to fly out there, can you take off some time to be together?"

I was actually a bit dazed at her offer. The last woman I'd thought I was in love with had broken off with me because I didn't have the money to keep her in the style to which she felt entitled. I knew Honey didn't have a big income, and she had a son to raise. That she cared enough to be willing to sacrifice just to spend time with me touched me deeply. It also showed me that maybe she was beginning to love me as much as I was falling head-over-heels in love with her.

Honey did fly out to join me, and we spent several wonderful days together. By the end of her visit, I knew this was the love of my life. But her son, job, and life were in Oklahoma. Mine was now in LA. When we could carve out a couple days, I flew back to Oklahoma to see her or she flew to see me. But as fast-paced as my life had become, our time together wasn't enough to build a solid relationship.

Then one day I was driving to an engagement in downtown LA when her name popped up on my caller ID. I answered the FaceTime call, "Hey, beautiful, how are you?"

The moment I saw her face without its usual big, happy smile, I knew something was wrong. I asked again, "Are you okay, Honey?"

In a soft, quiet voice, she responded, "Babe, I'm pregnant."

I froze, literally stunned into speechlessness. I didn't want to believe what I'd just heard. I was barely mature enough to be dating a single mom with a kid. I sure wasn't ready to be a dad! Besides, every dollar I had was tied up in getting our clothing line off the ground. How was I supposed to support a child, much less an entire household of four people? And being tied down to a family was not how I'd envisioned my great, new post-prison future.

Honey could already see my reaction. Finally, I got out the words, "No! We can't have a baby right now."

I might not have specifically used the word abortion, but she knew what I was suggesting. Without another word, she hung up. Crushed and unable to think straight, I drove home. All that night, I tossed and turned, trying to visualize myself as a father. The truth was, I just didn't want that responsibility. I'd lost a good bit of my twenties locked up. Now I was beginning to enjoy a new life as a young, single man. Maybe someday I'd be ready for a wife and family, but not now!

Honey wasn't sleeping either because she texted me in the middle of the night. She didn't hold back. She'd been so sure I was a kind, loving, gentle man who spoke about faith and GOD. That I could even suggest getting rid of our child made clear I was a fake and that she'd been absolutely wrong about me.

I couldn't argue because I could see her point of view. I was being a selfish, inconsiderate jerk. I was also acting just like the selfish jerk of a father I'd always sworn I'd never be like. When I'd met Honey's son, I'd asked myself how any father could walk away from his own flesh and blood, a child he'd been part of creating. Yet here I was contemplating something far worst—actually destroying my own child for my own convenience and freedom. Not even my biological father had stooped that low.

The next morning, I met Pops at the gym to train. I poured out what had happened, how I'd told Honey I didn't want a child, and how furious she'd been when I suggested an abortion. Pops told me to calm down and relax.

"Look, Abraham, a child is a blessing from GOD. I love you as a son, and one of the main reasons I've chosen to work with you is because I believe you are a great man overall with a great heart. And you'll be a great father. Maybe the timing isn't the best for everything we've planned. But we'll figure it out. GOD will be with you in this as he has been in everything else."

Right then and there, Pops and I prayed together and asked GOD to guide us. Then I called Honey, apologized for my initial selfish response, and committed myself to be there for her and our child every step of the way. I was still in a bit of panic mode, but I was suddenly also excited about having my first child. About doing everything good fathers do for their children. All the things Ken, Oscar, John Helstrom, Pops, and others had done for me.

Besides, how could I ever speak out again the message GOD had given me, everything I professed to stand for—Forever Faith, Mindset of Champions, GOD First, Others Second, Just Believe—if I walked away from my own child? I would be the biggest hypocrite of all time!

No, Pops was right. Regardless of our financial status, regardless of any challenges, we would be fine. After all, hadn't GOD shown his faithfulness over and over every step of my journey? Now he was sending another huge blessing into my life. I was going to be a father.

My beautiful wife and I have now been together almost a decade as of the writing of this book. Our precious son was born spring of 2012 in Tulsa, Oklahoma. I'm sure all of you fathers out there can relate to the confusion, fear, excitement, and joy of picking up your child for the first time. Pops was his first visitor in the recovery room. Our older son turned nine that same month and was delighted to welcome a new brother.

We were now a family of four.

CHAPTER TWENTY-NINE
MINDSET OF CHAMPIONS

FOR THE NEXT SEVERAL YEARS, HONEY and my two sons joined me in LA. The Forever Faith clothing line continued to grow with sales in over twenty countries. Community youth programs, elite prep schools, Latin American sports clubs, even teen Disney film stars were wearing Forever Faith clothing. So were fitness celebrities, pro wrestling stars, recording artists, and a growing number of NFL and NBA athletes. Forever Faith sponsored an anti-bullying campaign, providing event T-shirts that read "Stand Up, Speak Out, End Bullying."

I'd become a fitness name in my own right, winning several best-body competitions, giving TV, radio, print, and online interviews on my workout and nutrition routines, including *The Tonight Show* with Jay Leno. And not just English-language media. Since I'm bi-lingual, I soon found myself sharing my story on Spanish-language TV networks like Telemundo, one of the largest Spanish-language television networks on the planet, and Mundo Fox, Fox Broadcasting Company's Spanish-language affiliate. I also filmed a variety of comedy sketches with Tiny Lister as well as a music video and documentary.

Along with Pops, Honey was my biggest supporter in all of this. She has helped me grow so much as a man. I loved being a father and raising our two sons with her. They are a blessing from GOD. I came to realize that even the unexpected timing of our becoming a family was a blessing from GOD. Attractive, available women were as much a part of the entertainment and modeling world I now lived in as they'd been in the club scene that was my life before prison. With my track record, who knows if I'd have been able to stay strong against temptation without my beautiful wife and sons to keep me grounded.

Everything in my prison vision seemed to be coming true. I'd gone from a ten-by-ten prison cell to a one-bedroom Tulsa apartment to a 150,000 square-foot factory producing the Forever Faith brand for a global market. So long as I kept the faith and remained true to the promises I'd made GOD, I didn't think anything could bring me down.

Once again, I was wrong. To keep it short, our big-name manufacturing partners made some major mistakes of their own that landed them with a number of lawsuits. Their problems spilled over, and suddenly we were faced with our own lawsuit. This resulted in having to put production of the Forever Faith brand on hold until the lawsuit was settled.

It was a huge setback. Especially since it wasn't just me anymore. Now I had a family to support. But I wasn't crushed as I would have been a few years ago. Maybe because I've come to trust what GOD is doing in my life and understand that tough times are simply preparation for future opportunity. I can remember praying to GOD after finding out about the lawsuit and asking, "Please, Father GOD, settle all this and give us a second chance here. Bless us in this lawsuit so we can bless others."

Then I realized how silly that sounded because Father GOD had already given me a second chance at life, and I was living all the abundant blessings he'd given me. Freedom. A beautiful wife and family. Mentors like Pops. Food on the table and a roof over my head.

While we'd been building the Forever Faith brand, I'd asked Pops, "Why would GOD bless us with a multi-million-dollar business just like that?"

After all, I sure didn't deserve such an incredible blessing. Yes, I'd worked hard and done my part. That's the mindset of champions. But my prison vision coming true was GOD's doing, not mine. If GOD could bless me with so much, then it made sense he'd also send challenges to see if I'd keep the faith when setbacks came along, not just when things were going well.

That's in the Bible too. GOD tested Job. Joseph. Moses. King David. My namesake Abraham. Even Jesus. They all went through trials and testing of their faith while they were serving GOD. So who was I to think I shouldn't face trials as well as blessings? How could I expect GOD to continue blessing in the future if I was going to crumble and give up at every obstacle that came along?

"We didn't fail this time," I told Pops. "We didn't do anything wrong or make ungodly decisions. In fact, we've seen GOD do some incredible things. So I'm not going to give credit to the devil for this new setback. I'm going to have faith that this too is from GOD GOD part of his plan for our journey."

> "A true leader doesn't waste their time on the problem but focuses on the solution."
>
> —Abe Cruz

After much prayer, we decided to regroup back to Tulsa where Pops and Honey both had extended family and living costs were much lower. Scott Matlock, who'd taken a chance on me when I first got out of prison, hired me back at the gym without questions. Honey returned to her prior employment, which she eventually built into the successful independent business it is today. I also found work driving for UBER. All while still working with my Forever Faith team on the lawsuit and new opportunities.

I soon realized that our downsizing to Tulsa was its own blessing. After the constant fast-forward of LA, we now had time together as a couple and family. I could take our younger son to school each morning and pick him up in the afternoon. I could spend time with our older son, a teen now with only a few years left at home. While finances were tight, GOD always provided to pay the bills. I was also able to reconnect with old friends, including Jose Miranda.

But I also knew this wasn't all GOD had for us. Maybe the clothing line was on hold. But Forever Faith was not nor ever had been just a clothing line. It was a message. A mindset. And no lawsuit could put that on hold.

A few months into our return, I received a phone call from a fitness supplement company interested in having me represent their product. I tried the product, a topical workout gel called TC1, and absolutely loved it. They flew me to LA to film a commercial, and I ended up representing them for the next three years.

A month later, I received an invitation to co-host a fitness segment on a new Latino TV show *The Trend Talk*, hosted by Mexican-American journalists, news anchors, and producers Bel Hernandez and Naibe Reynoso. That project led to a number of interviews, fitness events, and speaking opportunities, including a fitness segment on *Fuerza TV*, a Tulsa-area Spanish-language TV/cable channel, and several features on *Up Close with Corey Taylor*, a TV talk show with Emmy-winning producer and motivational speaker Corey D. Taylor. I continued to speak as GOD opened doors at schools, churches, and sports programs.

Then in 2019, I received an invitation to participate in Exatlón, Telemundo's most popular reality show reaching millions of viewers in North America, Mexico, and throughout the Spanish-speaking world. The show pits a team of Latino fitness and sports celebrities, Team *Famosos* [Famous], against a team of top-ranked Latino civilian athletes, Team *Contendientes* [Contenders], in an elimination contest of various physical and mental challenges. Different contests take place in different Latin American countries. This one, *Exatlón Estados Unidos*, featured contestants from the United States.

I spent two months on the Famoso celebrity team before my own turn came to be eliminated. Many times in interviews and with my teammates, I was able to share my story from prison to transformation, giving all glory to GOD. Win or lose, I recognized that this experience alone fulfilled the vision I'd received in prison of sharing GOD's love to millions of people from all walks of life, regions of the world, and age demographics.

Only two major elements of my prison vision remained unfulfilled—writing a book and a movie that told my story. Through Jose Miranda, I met Jim Spargur, a highly-successful global business entrepreneur, and a close friend of theirs in the movie industry who has helped produce and distribute many award-winning faith-based movies such as *I Can Only Imagine*, *Soul Surfer*, *The End of the Spear*, and *The Pilgrims Progress*. Like Pops, they saw great potential in the Forever Faith message and have now joined the team as business partners and mentors. A Forever Faith movie is now in the workings. As for a book, you are holding that in your hands right now.

On April 2nd, 2019, after three long years of court actions, depositions, and repeated appeals, it took the judge less than a day to dismiss the lawsuit against Forever Faith in its entirety as being completely without merit. We now own the Forever Faith brand free and clear and are at liberty to relaunch every aspect of it.

So what exactly does that mean and what does the future hold? I have no idea! What I've learned during this time-out is that Forever Faith is not a brand or a product. It isn't about selling clothing, however inspirational, or getting on TV or any other professional success. It's about remaining faithful to the mission GOD called me to while on my face before him in a prison cell. It's about sharing GOD's love and message wherever and whatever GOD has for me next.

EPILOGUE
JUST BELIEVE!

Right now as I sit in the comfortable three-bedroom house God provided my beautiful wife, two sons, and me here in Tulsa, Oklahoma, I realize I've been blessed with everything I could possibly want. I'm so grateful for all that I have and where God has brought me to date. Whatever the future holds, my deepest prayer is that I can continue impacting lives God brings across my path in a positive, powerful way. So long as the core message of Forever Faith is being spread, that's what matters.

And I still have absolute faith that God has a big, bright, purpose-filled, God-blessed future ahead. I know this because every time one door has closed on this journey, I've seen God open ten more. That's just the way a loving Father is!

What else have I learned on this journey? I've learned that failure and losing are not the end but the beginning of a new mission and challenge.

I've learned that the impossible becomes possible with faith.

I've learned that you can grow up fatherless and in poverty, have all odds against you, even be a convicted felon, but when you hold on to faith, you will be a winner at any task you're given.

I've learned that when you feel weak, you've got to search deep inside and find that inner strength and motivation not to be a quitter no matter how badly you want to fall on your face and give up.

I've also learned that it isn't enough to just sit back and say you have faith. Like the Bible says, faith without works is dead. If you have true faith, you'll get up and go after those goals. You'll work hard. You'll sacrifice, demonstrate dedication, and keep commitments. You will also practice the principles of a true champion—treating others as you would wish to be treated, doing to others as Jesus would do.

If you follow those guidelines, if in your heart, mind, soul, and spirit you are doing everything in the best manner you can possibly do, then you are a winner. You are a champion. It doesn't matter if maybe you lose one particular game, employment opportunity, or professional accomplishment. The good thing about life is that there is no scoreboard. We might lose today, but tomorrow we have another opportunity to play again.

> "If faith no bigger than a mustard seed can move mountains, imagine what faith the size of a mountain could do!" —Abe Cruz

Let me make clear here that the Forever Faith message is not for the pessimist but for the optimist. It's for the person who doesn't let pain, grief, or past mistakes define them. The person who is willing to accept failure and use it as a motivational tool for betterment.

I mentioned clear back when I introduced myself that Forever Faith is about having the mindset of a champion. About becoming the very best version of yourself in every area of life. Not just spiritually, though that is a priority. But also physically, mentally, emotionally, socially, financially, etc. And the root of that is putting GOD first because GOD *is* the ultimate champion.

Once you have that mindset of a champion, every area of your life will improve. Instead of seeing problems, you will see challenges. And challenges are simply steps to solutions. Instead of getting frustrated or upset when something goes wrong, the mindset of a champion figures it out, asks for help, deals with the situation, and moves on.

I recently received a message from a prison inmate. He reminded me that we'd been in Oklahoma City County Jail together, where I'd gotten him hooked on working out. A friend had shared with him what GOD was doing in my life. He wrote that he was reaching out to me because everyone in jail had dreams, but I'd actually made mine happen. He wanted to know how he could do the same.

My answer to him is the same I give to you. It all comes down to faith. As I said at the beginning, if faith could save my life, it can save yours too. If faith can make my GOD-dreams from prison a reality, it can do the same for yours.

It just takes a little bit of faith. In fact, Jesus once said if we have faith no bigger than a mustard seed, we can move mountains. A mustard seed is pretty small, so just imagine what faith the size of a mountain could do.

Mindset-of-Champions faith.

Forever faith.

Just believe!

ABOUT THE AUTHORS

Abe Cruz is a successful businessman, renowned athlete, and motivational speaker. He is the founder and president of *Forever Faith*, a company through which he carries his message of hope and inspiration through fitness products, clothing and events, reaching millions of people around the world. To learn more, visit **www.foreverfaith.com**.

Award-winning investigative author and journalist Jeanette Windle has lived and worked in North, Central and South America, and has visited more than forty countries on five continents. Her experiences have given birth to more than twenty-one fiction and nonfiction books, including *Forgiven*, the story of Torri Roberts and the Amish school massacre, and *All Saints*, now a Sony movie.

www.FOREVERFAITH.com
MINDSET OF CHAMPIONS

APPAREL
Tees | Hoodies | Tanks | Leggings | Joggers

NEW! FOREVERFAITH FITNESS CBD topical creams for Anti-inflammation, Healing, Recovery & Deeper Sleep!

www.FOREVERFAITH.com

MINDSET OF CHAMPIONS

Made in the USA
Middletown, DE
04 April 2021